ST. TERESA OF CALCUTTA

St. Teresa
of Calcutta
MISSIONARY, MOTHER, MYSTIC

KERRY
WALTERS

Franciscan
MEDIA
Cincinnati, Ohio

Cover and book design by Mark Sullivan
Cover image via Wikimedia I Manfred Ferrari

LIBRARY OF CONGRESS CATALOGING-IN-PUBLICATION DATA
Names: Walters, Kerry S., author.
Title: St. Teresa of Calcutta : missionary, mother, mystic / Kerry Walters.
Description: Cincinnati : Franciscan Media, 2016. I Includes bibliographical
references.
Identifiers: LCCN 2016024460 I ISBN 9781632531247 (trade paper)
Subjects: LCSH: Teresa, Mother, 1910-1997. I Missionaries of
Charity—Biography. I Nuns—India—Biography.
Classification: LCC BX4406.5.Z8 W35 2016 I DDC 271/.97—dc23
LC record available at https://lccn.loc.gov/2016024460

ISBN 978-1-63253-124-7

Published by Franciscan Media
28 W. Liberty St.
Cincinnati, OH 45202
www.FranciscanMedia.org

Printed in the United States of America.
Printed on acid-free paper.
16 17 18 19 20 5 4 3 2 1

To Fred Mahan
Dear Friend and Fellow Traveler

All we do—our prayer, our work, our suffering—is for Jesus. Our life has no other reason or motivation. This is a point many people do not understand. I serve Jesus twenty-four hours a day. Whatever I do is for Him. And He gives me strength. I love Him in the poor and the poor in Him, but always the Lord comes first. Whenever a visitor comes to our house, I take him to the chapel to pray awhile. I tell Him, "let us first greet the Master of the house. Jesus is here."[1]

—St. Teresa of Calcutta

contents

BECOMING HOLY

"Jesus wants us to be holy."[1]

I n his autobiographical *The Seven Story Mountain*, Thomas
Merton remembers a conversation with poet Robert Lax.
The two friends were strolling in Greenwich Village shortly
after Merton's conversion to Christianity when Lax suddenly
asked: "What do you want to be, anyway?"

Taken by surprise, Merton rather lamely answered, "I don't
know; I guess what I want is to be a good Catholic." Without
hesitating, Lax shot back, "What you *should* say is that you
want to be a saint!" Bewildered, Merton asked, "How do you
expect me to become a saint?" "By wanting to," replied Lax.[2]

Merton's friend was right. Our deepest, most heartfelt desire,
even if we are not quite aware of it, is to grow ever more saintly
or holy, to enter ever more intimately into relationship with
God. All our other desires are either expressions or perversions
of this wellspring.

Mother Teresa, called by many the "saint of the gutters," or
"saint of the slums," because of her ministry to the poor, recognized her desire for holiness at a young age. Even though she
put it aside for three or four of her teenage years, she rediscov-
ered it by the time she was eighteen. The desire never deserted
her, although, as we now know, she often felt that God had.

For the rest of her days, her one goal was to live a holy life, a life pleasing to God and of service to suffering humanity, even when God seemed absent.

And she succeeded. So obvious was Mother Teresa's sanctity that immediately after her death on September 5, 1997, her admirers began advocating for her canonization. Pope John Paul II was initially reluctant to speed up the process, but his admiration for Mother Teresa was so great that he eventually agreed. The official investigation of her life, a necessary step toward canonization, began less than two years after her death, leading to her beatification in October 2003. In his homily on that occasion, Pope John Paul II said, "I am personally grateful to this courageous woman, whom I have always felt beside me." She was, he noted, "an icon of the Good Samaritan."[3] Thirteen years later, on September 4, 2016, Pope Francis concluded the process when he declared Mother Teresa a saint, naming her forever as St. Teresa of Calcutta.

Most of us, of course, will always think of her simply and affectionately as Mother Teresa, the diminutive nun whose life and ministry to the poor was captured in thousands of iconic photographs. She's always dressed the same, in the white sari with blue trim that is the habit of the Missionaries of Charity, the order Teresa founded and led for nearly a half-century. Another blue-bordered scarf covers her head and brow, and on her left shoulder, next to her heart, a small crucifix is pinned.

Teresa's face is incredibly lined; even as a middle-aged nun she began to look older than her years. Her fingers are thick, blunted from years of scrubbing floors and toilets, and her hands' wrinkled skin looks like elephant hide. Her feet are small, with toes almost grotesquely misshapen from decades of wearing ill-fitting and secondhand sandals. She's a small woman, just barely 4 feet, 11 inches tall. Age and labor have bent her back, making her even shorter. Toward the end of her life, she sometimes looked bent double.

In the familiar photographs, Teresa's expression is alternately somber, reflective, contemplative, exhausted, and at times even angry. But occasionally the camera catches her when she's smiling or joyfully laughing. She has a wonderful smile. It lights up her face and warms the heart of whoever sees it, even if only through the one-dimensional flatness of a photo.

In contrast to the thousands of photographic images of her as Mother Teresa of the Missionaries of Charity, there are only a few sepia-colored ones taken of Anjezë Gonxhe Bojaxhiu, the girl who grew up to become the saint of the gutters. In one of them, she poses with friends while holding an open umbrella. In another, taken shortly before she left home for India, she stares rather pensively at the camera. Perhaps she's trying to catch a glimpse of her future.

These youthful photos, taken in the 1920s, are extraordinary. They reveal that Anjezë has thick, dark hair and a high, graceful forehead, both of which disappear forever behind a veil when she becomes a nun. Despite her short stature, she stands tall and straight. But there's one unmistakable feature that remains constant in the early and later photos: her eyes. There's something penetratingly luminous about them, as if they're more than capable of reflecting both sheer joy and intolerable suffering. They are eyes, one's almost tempted to say, which have seen God and are alert for another glimpse of the

Divine. But they're also eyes that have witnessed some of the worst suffering—disease, poverty, starvation, scorn, and indifference—that can afflict human beings.

If our eyes are indeed the windows of the soul, as some believe, the soul of the girl Anjezë and the woman Mother Teresa is holy indeed. And it's that holiness, that living commitment to conform her human will to God's, the same goal that Robert Lax recommended to Thomas Merton, which captivated the world during her lifetime and continues to hold us spellbound today. In examining Teresa's life, her works, and her spirituality, we learn how to grow into our birthright as creatures made in the likeness of God. She teaches us how to open our eyes to see with her clarity.

Whenever people asked her what sustained her throughout her hard years of service, she often quoted St. Augustine: "Fill yourself first [with God], and only then will you be able to give to others."[4] God's "perfect will" for us, she always insisted, is that we become holy, asking divine grace to fuel our desires and efforts in that direction. "He has chosen us; we have not first chosen him."[5] But we also have our part to play by surrendering to that divine stirring, which in effect means conforming our will to God's, such that we, like the apostle Paul, can say that Christ lives in us. As Mother Teresa counseled her Sisters, "Remember the work is not ours and we must not spoil it. That would be a great injustice to God because the work is his."[6]

This surrender is what the Roman Catholic priest and author Henri Nouwen often referred to as "downward mobility," the will to repudiate pride and ego in order to love God and our fellow humans. This ideal of selflessness, embraced by Christian mystics such as St. Paul, St. Francis of Assisi, and St. Teresa of Avila, is a downward movement in two senses: first, because it is a rejection of the upward mobility of economic success and worldly power, second because it is an inward withdrawal to discern God's stirrings in our deepest core.

And how do we achieve downward mobility? "Not by reading plenty of books," Mother Teresa said, "or by listening to many words, but by accepting humiliations" in a prayerful and even grateful way, accepting what comes our way and letting go of any bitterness or disappointment.[7]

> The words "I want to be holy" mean: I will divest myself of everything that is not of God; I will divest myself and empty my heart of material things. I will renounce my own will, my inclinations, my whims, my fickleness; and I will become a generous slave to God's will.[8]

It's possible that Nouwen's recommendation of downward mobility was actually inspired by a conversation he once had with Mother Teresa. He tells us that when he met her, he began pouring out a litany of worries about his spiritual life. Teresa patiently listened to him for ten minutes or so, and then quietly said, "Well, when you spend one hour a day adoring your Lord and never do anything which you know is wrong...you will be fine!"[9]

The first step in becoming holy, then, according to the saint of the slums, is to will to be holy by practicing the self-emptying of downward mobility. Mother Teresa often taught this lesson in a characteristically simple way. Holding up all ten of her fingers and ticking them off one by one, she would say: "I will, I want, with God's blessing, to be holy."[10] And the route to achieving that is regular prayerful adoration of the Lord.

The second step to holiness, profligate love, comes a lot easier once the first step is taken. Emptying ourselves of our pride and our me-centered addiction to instant gratification clears our spiritual vision to recognize our sisters and brothers as the lovable creatures they are. No longer enslaved by our egos, we're able to notice and touch the wounds of humanity, and this breaks our hearts of stone and replaces them with God's compassion.

We can again turn to Thomas Merton who, in a well-known description of an epiphany he experienced while standing on a street corner, beautifully captures the new way of looking at the world that love brings.

> In Louisville, at the corner of Fourth and Walnut, in the center of the shopping district, I was suddenly over-whelmed with the realization that I loved all those people, that they were mine and I theirs, that we could not be alien to one another even though we were total strangers. It was like waking from a dream of separate-ness, of spurious self-isolation in a special world, the world of renunciation and supposed holiness.... This sense of liberation from an illusory difference was such a relief and such a joy to me that I almost laughed out loud.... I have the immense joy of being man, a member of a race in which God Himself became incarnate. As if the sorrows and stupidities of the human condition could overwhelm me, now I realize what we all are. And if only everybody could realize this! But it cannot be explained.

There is no way of telling people that they are all
walking around shining like the sun.[11]

There's no reason to suppose that Mother Teresa had read this
passage, or even knew who Thomas Merton was. But her entire
life was an exercise in helping people rejected and broken by
society to see themselves as radiant carriers of God's likeness.
That's certainly how she saw them.

The third step to holiness follows naturally from love: putting
our love for God and our fellow humans into action, dedicating
ourselves to a life of service with a commitment so strong that
it stretches toward the very heavens. Mother Teresa puts it in a
breathtakingly audacious way: "Christ tells us to aim very high,
not to be like Abraham or David or any of the saints, but to be
like our heavenly Father."[12]

The key to sustaining love in action, Teresa taught, is learning
to see Christ in everyone. She once said that just as a priest sees
Christ in a consecrated host, so we need to see Christ in all
of the disguises, be they resplendent or distressing, he wears.
When we willingly undertake the works of mercy out of love
for those we serve, we cleave to Christ.

If her luminous eyes and calm face tell us anything, it's that the
girl Anjezë Gonxhe Bojaxhiu had already, by the grace of God,
intuited much of this even before she became a nun. What takes
most of us a lifetime (and more!) to grasp, God gave her when
she was still young. Her self-emptying love and service grew
richer as the years unfolded until she discerned, two decades
after taking the habit, her true calling in life: selfish service to
people of the slums and gutters. But the trajectory of her road
to holy sainthood, a trajectory that can be visually traced in

photographs of her that span eighty years, clearly starts in her youth.

So it's there that we'll begin.

chapter one

A SKOPJE CHILDHOOD

"We were a very united and happy family."[1]

The woman who once observed that there would be no need for "tanks and generals" if only people learned to see the image of God in their neighbors entered the world in a region bristling with strife.[2] From the moment of her birth until she left home at the age of eighteen, the life of Anjezë Gonxhe Bojaxhiu, the future Teresa of Calcutta, was set against the backdrop of war.

Anjezë was born on August 26, 1910, in the city of Skopje, Kosovo, a predominately Serbian town in the crumbling Ottoman Empire. Shortly before her birth, ethnic Albanians in Kosovo launched an unsuccessful bid for independence. This revolt was followed by two regional wars that resulted in a redrawing of borders that finally created an Albanian state. Shortly afterward, in 1914, World War I erupted, engulfing all of Europe in a nightmare of violence that once again destabilized the Balkans.

Both of her parents were ethnic Albanians whom Mother Teresa remembered as being devoted to one another. Her mother "used to be very busy the whole day, but as soon as the evening came, she moved very quickly to get ready to meet my father.... What a tremendous, delicate love she had for him."[3]

Nikola, Anjezë's father, was an outspoken advocate of Albanian statehood. Since Skopje remained in Serbian territory after the creation of Albania, Nikola, a successful businessman as well as a city councilor, began agitating for the town's incorporation into the new nation. In the process, he earned the respect of many of his fellow displaced Albanians, but he also made some powerful political enemies. When he died suddenly in 1919, many people suspected he'd been poisoned by Serbian nationalists. He was only forty-five. His youngest daughter wasn't yet ten.

Nikola's widow, Drana, and her three children, Anjezë (8), Lazar (11), and Aga (15), were left destitute. Nikola had been a good provider, but when he died, his assets were embezzled by a business partner. Drana struggled to keep the family together by taking in sewing and embroidery work. Despite the family's precarious finances, however, she insisted that whoever came to her door hungry would be welcome to share a meal. She taught her children "never to eat a single mouthful unless you are sharing it with others."[4] It was a lesson Anjezë never forgot. As Mother Teresa recalled, "She taught us to love God and to love our neighbor."[5] Brother Lazar agreed. According to him, Drana "never allowed any of the poor people who came to our door to leave empty-handed. When we [children] would look at her strangely, she would say, 'Keep in mind that even those who are not our blood relatives, even if they are poor, are still our brethren.'"[6]

It's not surprising that Mother Teresa once described her mother as a "holy woman."[7]

Drana's commitment to hospitality for the poor sprang from her deep faith. Although most Albanians were either Orthodox or Muslim, the Bojaxhiu family was Roman Catholic, and daily prayers at home, regular attendance at Sacred Heart, the town's only Catholic church, and pilgrimages to holy shrines were the norm. Lazar occasionally grumbled about his mother's and sisters' piety. They "seemed to live as much in the church as they did at home," he recalled as an adult. "They were always involved with the choir, the religious services, and missionary topics."[8]

The Bojaxhiu women were also involved in the parish choir, a natural outlet because the entire family was musically talented. Drana insisted that each of her children learn to play an instrument. Anjezë chose the mandolin while still a small child. She also had a good voice, and was one of two girls in the parish sometimes invited to sing solos during services.

Anjezë was the baby of the family, and like many youngest children was probably coddled more than her two older siblings. Her nickname was Gonxha, a play on her middle name that means "flower bud." She was by temperament a quiet and somewhat introspective girl, but her shyness was less of a concern for Drana than her physical constitution. The town of Skopje is located in a valley, and a river runs through its heart. The thick air of hot and humid summers gave Anjezë a persistent cough that convinced Drana the child wasn't long for the world. On top of that, she also suffered from the periodic chills and fever of malaria, a chronic condition that would plague her for the rest of her life and come close to killing her when she was old and frail.

Partly to get Anjezë out of the valley and into the cooler mountains, but mainly because of Drana's deep faith, she and her children made an annual pilgrimage to the chapel of Our Lady of the Black Mountain in the mining town of Letnica. In later years, Mother Teresa was convinced that the intercessions of the Madonna of Letnica accounted for her vocation. "It was at the feet of our Lady of Letnica where I first heard the divine call.... I remember the afternoon of her feast of the Assumption. I was praying with a lighted candle in my hands and singing in my heart, full of joy inside, when I took the decision to wholly devote myself to God through religious life."[9] The four-hundred-year-old wooden Madonna at whose feet Anjezë prayed was blackened with age even in 1928. Every Feast of the Assumption, thousands of Roman Catholics still visit Letnica to venerate the Black Madonna. Many of them walk miles to the chapel in bare feet or with pebbles in their shoes as acts of penitence, just as pilgrims did in Anjezë's day.

Anjezë's commitment to her faith quickly grew as strong as her mother's. Although she attended the state school in Skopje— she was a fairly good pupil, but not as dedicated to her studies as her older sister Aga—her real education was under the tutelage of Fr. Franjo Jambrekovic, a Croatian Jesuit assigned to Sacred Heart. Jambrekovic gave lectures to the parish on a number of topics, sacred as well as secular, created a parish library, and organized a club dedicated to the Virgin Mary for the parish girls.

As the girls' spiritual director, Jambrekovic's spiritual instruction inevitably centered on the Spiritual Exercises of Ignatius of Loyola, founder of the Society of Jesus, whose members were known as Jesuits. The girls were encouraged, for example, to practice the daily examination of conscience required of Jesuits.

They were also trained in the Ignatian technique of imagina-tively placing themselves in different biblical scenes, an exercise aimed at helping them think less abstractly about the faith. We have no record of the scenes into which Anjezë placed herself. But given her mother's insistence on feeding hungry wayfarers, it's likely that the story of the Feeding of the Five Thousand, found in all four Gospels, was one of them.

Like many religious youngsters, Anjezë went through a (fortunately) short period of judgmental primness. Her brother Lazar remembered that, for a time, she regularly scolded him for eating before receiving Communion. But helped by the gentle guidance of her mother and Fr. Jambrekovic's instruc-tion, she discovered at quite a young age that she had a voca-tion to the religious life. The conviction came to her on one of the family pilgrimages to the Letnica shrine. "I was only twelve years old and lived at home with my parents when I first felt the desire to become a nun.... We had very good priests who were helping the boys and girls to follow their vocation according to the call of God. It was then that I first knew I had a vocation to the poor."[10] Drana, alarmed that her daughter's physical frailty wasn't up to the rigors of convent life, dissuaded her. It's not clear if Fr. Jambrekovic likewise discouraged Anjezë. The like-liest guess is that he recommended she test her sense of calling by waiting a few years.

That's exactly what she did. She continued her religious instruction, her regular attendance at Mass, her participation in family prayers, and her retreats. Interestingly, despite her deep piety, she grew less enthusiastic about her call, finally deciding that it had been an impulse rather than a genuine message from God.

Anjezë may well have remained in Skopje her entire life as a wife and mother who dabbled in music and writing. She was, after all, exceptionally fond of her mandolin and her singing, and she'd already published a couple of articles in the local newspaper. But when she was in her mid-teens, she became enthralled by stories about serving Christ in India, relayed through letters written by Jesuit friends of Fr. Jambrekovic's who were missionaries there. He in turn shared their letters with his congregation. Years later, Mother Teresa recalled that the missionaries' tales, "used to give us the most beautiful descriptions about the experiences they had with the people, and especially the children, in India."[11] She found them excitingly exotic.

Anjezë's interest in India might also have been sparked by newspaper accounts of a middle-aged Indian barrister named Mohandas Gandhi who had struggled against apartheid in South Africa before returning to his native land in 1915. Gandhi's arrival in India was greeted by cheering crowds and official honors, including a gold medal in the king's 1915 honor list for his anti-apartheid efforts. Reading about Gandhi's triumphant return to India only made the missionaries' tales even more intriguing.

By the time she was eighteen, the sense of vocation Anjezë had felt six years earlier returned. When it did, she felt, not surprisingly given her interest in India, that God was calling her to bring spiritual and material comfort to the poor in foreign lands. Years afterward, looking back on her youthful redis-covery of a vocation, Mother Teresa said, "I've never doubted even for a second that I've done the right thing: it was the will of God. It was his choice."[12] In later life, she would often point skyward when asked about why she became a nun. She meant that God, not she, had determined her destiny.

It may have been God's wish that she become a missionary, but it wasn't Drana's. When Anjezë shared the news of her vocation with her mother, Drana once again tried to dissuade her. One of Mother Teresa's biographers suggests that Drana refused her consent this second time in order to test her daughter's resolve.[13] Perhaps. But in a family as close as the Bojaxhius were, grief at losing her youngest daughter, probably forever given the distance between India and Skopje, may also have influenced Drana. She knew that if Anjezë did join a missionary order there was a good chance the two would never see one another again.

As things turned out, her fear was well-founded. After leaving Skopje in 1928, Anjezë's only contact for the rest of her life with her mother was through the post. After the Balkans came under Soviet domination in the wake of World War II, most letters sent by mother and daughter were held up or simply lost before arriving at their destination. Mother Teresa tried several times over the years to return to her home to visit Drana and Aga. But her work in India kept her too busy to travel, and the restrictions of the communists would've kept her out of the country anyway. Teresa was never to see her mother again.

The pain that Drana felt at the prospect of losing a daughter caused her to shut herself up in her bedroom for a full twenty-four hours, during which she must have done some prayerful wrestling with God. When she finally emerged from the room, she was reconciled, howsoever sadly, to her daughter's wish to become a missionary. She gave Anjezë her blessing, but added the rather intimidating advice that anything short of whole-hearted dedication would displease God. "Put your hand in his hand," Drana told her daughter, "and walk all alone with him."[14] Perhaps this was a last-minute effort to frighten her youngest daughter into reconsidering her plan. If so, it didn't work.

Drana wasn't the only member of the family who disapproved of Anjezë's vocation. Her brother, Lazar, also thought it a bad idea, although apparently for reasons different than Drana's. Lazar, never comfortable with the family's piety, had been abroad for some years, studying first in Austria and then in a military academy in Albania. As elder brothers are sometimes inclined to do, he was overprotective of his youngest sister, believing that she was making a bad mistake, and he wrote her a letter to that effect. In replying to him, the family's frail "flower bud" revealed that she could give as good as she got. "You think you are important, because you are an officer serving a king [Zog I of Albania] with two million subjects. But I am serving the King of the whole world."[15]

Now that Anjezë was confident that her sense of vocation was genuine—Fr. Jambrekovic reassured her that the joy she felt was a sure sign of God's calling—the task was to discern what religious order of missionary nuns would best suit her talents and temperament.

Once again the parish priest's advice proved invaluable. He recommended the Institute of the Blessed Virgin Mary, an order of missionary nuns especially dedicated to educating young people. Commonly called the Sisters of Loreto after a Marian shrine in Italy that the order's founder, Venerable Mary Ward, frequently visited, the nuns ran several schools in India.

As soon as she learned about them, Anjezë was eager to join, and she lost no time in writing to the Loreto Mother Superior requesting admission. Her letter's innocent earnestness is touching.

> Be so kind to hear my sincere desire. I want to join your Society, so that one day I may become a missionary sister, and work for Jesus who died for us all.... I don't have any special conditions, I only want to be in the missions, and for everything else I surrender myself completely to the good God's disposal.[16]

To her great joy, Anjezë soon received a positive reply to her letter. But before she could be admitted to postulancy, she had to travel to Paris for a formal interview. On the evening of September 26, 1928, exactly one month after her eighteenth birthday, Anjezë, Drana, and Aga boarded a train for Zagreb, about eight hundred kilometers north of Skopje. Once there, final tearful good-byes were said, and Anjezë, in the company of another young woman seeking admittance to the Sisters of Loreto, boarded a second train bound for Paris. On the basis of their interviews there, both of them were accepted as Loreto postulants.

* * *

Before they could embark for India, they had to be schooled in the spirituality of their order and, just as importantly, begin tutelage in English, the language not only of the Sisters of Loreto but also of most educated Indians. So Anjezë spent six weeks at Loreto Abbey, located in a suburb of Dublin, taking a crash course in a language she'd never heard before. It had to have been an intense immersion, but Anjezë was clever and afire to become a missionary. So she applied herself, and by the time she set sail for India from Dublin on December 1, 1928, she had already picked up the rudiments of English.

There's little doubt that leaving home was hard for Anjezë. Even Lazar, her sometimes cynical and always worldly brother, nostalgically remembered that the family had always been close, and even more so after Nikola's death. But three factors made the departure less painful for Anjezë than it might've been. First, she was confident that this was what God wanted of her. Second, the sheer sense of adventure she felt at the prospect of going to what must have seemed a truly exotic land was exhilarating, even if also a bit frightening. Finally, the destructiveness of World War I, the misnamed "War to End All Wars," had left the Balkans in economic, geopolitical, and cultural tatters. It was a good time to leave.

The long voyage to India was uneventful. Anjezë celebrated Christmas on board with her fellow Loreto postulant and three Franciscan missionary sisters, but there was no Mass because none of the passengers were priests. Although Anjezë felt an excited sense of liberation now that she had finally embarked for India, she couldn't help but mourn for the childhood and family she was leaving behind. While aboard ship, she expressed some of her sorrow in plaintive verse. "I'm leaving my dear house," she wrote, forsaking friends and family for a "distant shore." She entreated God to accept her sacrifice of departing from her loved ones, perhaps forever, and asked in return only that she be allowed to "save at least one soul."[17]

The intermingling of excitement and loneliness revealed in Anjezë's verse would continue for the rest of her life. She never lost her zeal for missionary work, and never doubted her calling. But as her posthumously published letters revealed, she suffered from an intense loneliness during the last fifty years of her life that no amount of work or prayer would alleviate. As we'll see in a later chapter, she once confessed that if she ever became a saint, she would be one of darkness.

chapter two

LORETO

"I wanted to be a missionary."[1]

A young woman's dream of missionary work in a foreign and exotic country is one thing, but the reality is often something quite different. For Anjezë, the brutality of Indian poverty, encountered for the first time when her ship made a stop at the Tamil city of Madras, was shocking.

As she explored the streets of Madras during the brief layover there, she witnessed scenes of misery that rivaled any suffering she'd seen back home. Entire families were homeless and jobless. They lived in the open air and managed to just survive through begging. At one point, Anjezë witnessed a Hindu funeral, and was horrified by the lines of color the dead man's mourners had painted on his face. By the time she returned to the ship for the final leg of its journey, any naïvely romantic fantasies about life in India she might've entertained had begun to vanish.

It was nearly seven weeks before Anjezë and her fellow postulant finally arrived at the port of Calcutta in West Bengal, then and now one of the most densely populated areas in the world. At least initially, the teeming and noisy metropolis can overwhelm Western visitors, and it's entirely likely that young Anjezë and her companion had the same response. But they hadn't long to be bewildered, because in mid-January 1929 they were

13

whisked to the Loreto Novitiate located 630 kilometers north in Darjeeling, a town nestled in the Himalayan foothills.

The India in which Anjezë would spend the rest of her life was still a British colony. Colonial officers, including the viceroy, regularly retreated to the cooler climate of Darjeeling to escape the intense summer heat of Calcutta and New Delhi. So for all practical purposes, Darjeeling was a resort town four months of the year. Garden parties, cricket, polo, dances, and stage productions entertained senior British officials as well as the handful of maharajas who also summered there.

The primary mission of the Loreto Sisters was and still is teaching. Accordingly, the Darjeeling novitiate trained novices in the spirituality of the order as well as in pedagogical technique, although the latter seems to have been accomplished primarily by requiring novices to teach in the school attached to the novitiate for two hours each day. They were also required to learn one of the native Indian languages. Anjezë, still mastering English, also immersed herself in Bengali. She eventually became fluent in both (earning for a time the nickname "Bengali Teresa"), and also picked up a bit of Hindi along the way.

The months at the novitiate passed quickly, and Anjezë took her initial vows of poverty, chastity, and obedience in late March 1931, when she was still only twenty years old. The new name she settled on for her religious life was revealing. She gave up her birth name to become Sister Mary Teresa of the Child Jesus. She chose it because she had a special devotion to Thérèse of Lisieux, canonized only three years earlier by Pope Pius XI, the same pontiff who had encouraged European Christians, including the Jesuit priests whose epistolary accounts of their ministry in India had so impressed Anjezë, to serve as missionaries throughout the world. Thérèse had been canonized in record time, a mere twenty-eight years after her death. Mother Teresa would best that record when Pope Francis declared her a saint only nineteen years after her 1997 death.

Anjezë felt especially close to Thérèse of Lisieux. For one thing, they had similar nicknames: "little bud" and "little flower." Additionally, before she entered a cloistered Carmelite convent, Thérèse, like Anjezë, had longed to travel to exotic lands as a missionary. (As a nun, Thérèse took special care to pray for Roman Catholic priests and nuns who worked abroad. After her canonization, she was declared patron of missionaries.) Finally, both women came from intensely pious families, both had lost a parent, both had suffered from ill health in their youth, and both, as youngest children, were a bit coddled (although Thérèse significantly more so than Anjezë).

But the most significant bond between the two women was a spiritual one. The Little Flower had taught that God doesn't expect great deeds from all or even most of us, but is more than satisfied with the "little" acts of love we perform on a daily basis. The Kingdom of Heaven is reached little by little, not by storm. For the rest of her life, and especially after she left the Sisters of Loreto to live among and minister to the poor, Teresa was convinced that her call was to serve individuals, not large groups. She served her Lord step by step, day by day, and person by person.

Why "Teresa" rather than "Thérèse"? The reason was simple enough: There was already a sister who had changed her baptismal name to Thérèse. So, Anjezë "chose the name Teresa for my religious vows. But it wasn't the name of the great Teresa of Avila. I chose the name of Teresa of the Little Flower, Thérèse of Lisieux."[2] She would be known as Sister Teresa for the next six years, changing from "Sister" to "Mother" when she took final vows.

Shortly after her initial vows, Teresa was sent back to Calcutta, assigned to the Loreto orphanage and school compound located in the neighborhood of Entally. At the time, Entally was one of the most poverty-stricken areas in Calcutta, avoided by Europeans and Indian Brahmins alike. The people who lived there were mostly members of the despised caste known as Dalits or "untouchables." Consigned to the lowest rung in the caste system, Dalits scraped together pitiful livings by performing work that no member of a higher caste would think about doing: cleaning public toilets, picking up refuse from the streets, slaughtering animals in abattoirs. Thousands of unskilled peasants forced off their lands by unscrupulous landlords or bad harvests regularly flooded into the slums of Calcutta, joining the ranks of the Dalits and often winding up reduced to beggary.

The Loreto compound in which Teresa lived and worked was founded in 1845. It consisted of several buildings within high walls that shut out the noisy misery of the streets. Between the school and the orphanage, the nuns there served some five hundred children.

Sister Teresa was initially assigned to St. Mary's, one of the compound schools, tasked with teaching geography and history, subjects she particularly enjoyed. The compound boasted grass, trees, and adequate food and water in contrast to the squalor outside its walls, but the Sisters' working days were long and hard. Prayers and Mass in the early morning were followed by a quick breakfast and six solid hours of teaching. Late afternoons and evenings were devoted to helping children with their studies, supervising their recreation, and feeding them. Only then could the Sisters say evening prayers and fall, exhausted, into bed. But Teresa, although never in robust health, did everything expected of her conscientiously and joyfully. One of the Sisters with whom she worked remembered her as a "very hard worker. Very. Up to time on this, up to time on that. She never wanted to shirk anything, she was always ready. Always a very pious person, she was just herself.... She fitted in very ready."[3]

After four years at St. Mary's, Teresa asked to be reassigned to St. Teresa's, a primary school on the other side of the compound walls. Walking there brought her into daily contact with the poverty, squalor, disease, and crime everywhere apparent in Entally. What she saw filled her "full of anguish." "It is not possible," she wrote at the time, "to find worse poverty."[4] More than once she must have come close to despair at the miserable living conditions of the children she taught. The defining ministry of Loreto was to reduce poverty by giving children the chance to escape it through education. But it was hard to see how teaching Dalit children to read, write, and do simple sums would ever improve their lot in life. Educated or not, they remained on the bottom rung of the Indian caste system.

Teresa never wavered in her fidelity to the Loreto vision, even after she left the order. But she gradually began to wonder if teaching alone was what God wanted of her. It was brought home to her time and again during her years at St. Teresa's that children can't learn much when they haven't eaten for two or three days, or when they suffer from an infection or illness brought about by living on the streets. So beginning during her time at St. Teresa's and continuing when she returned to the Loreto compound in 1937, she began visiting Entally's poor on Sundays, offering them friendship and doing her best to scrounge basic necessities of life for them. She also began visiting them when they were in hospital, although most Dalits who were ill either died on the streets of Entally or recovered without the benefit of medical aid. What especially struck her was the intense gratitude they felt simply because she treated them as human beings.

"I cannot help them," she wrote at the time, "because I do not have anything, but I go to give them joy.... [One] poor mother [she visited] did not utter even a word of complaint about her poverty. It was very painful for me, but at the same time I was very happy when I saw that they are happy because I visit them. Finally, the mother said to me, 'Oh, Ma, come again! Your smile brought sun into this house!'"[5]

The lesson she gleaned from such visits, that the poor were just as famished for love and dignity as for rice, remained with her the rest of her life, and would become a cornerstone conviction of the Missionaries of Charity.

The seeds of Teresa's insight that the poor hungered for love as well as food had been sown years earlier by her mother, Drana. Drana had planted them when she cared for a woman named File, who apparently suffered from some kind of skin disease that others, including her own relatives, found so repulsive that they abandoned her. In a letter to her daughter, Drana remembered poor File in words that could only have reinforced Teresa's desire to show untouchables love. "She was covered in sores," Drana wrote, "but what caused her far more suffering was the knowledge that she was all alone in the world. We did what we could for her but the worst thing was not the sores but the fact that her family had forgotten her."[6]

On May 24, 1937, on retreat in Darjeeling, Teresa took final vows as a Sister of Loreto. Henceforth she would be known as Mother Teresa, as was the custom in her order. But despite the joy she took in her work, Teresa remained restless. In a letter to Fr. Jambrekovic, she expressed her ongoing struggle to offer everything to Christ. "I want to be only all for Jesus [but] many times this goes upside-down—so my most reverend 'I' gets the most important place." But regardless of how often her "I" got in the way, she also felt a great desire to "drink the chalice to the last drop.... Everything is for Jesus; so like that everything is beautiful, even though it is difficult."[7] To drink the last drop: allusions to thirst, hers as well as Jesus's, began to appear with regularity in Mother Teresa's letters.

She was beginning to formulate what would become one of the pillars of her spirituality: that Christ thirsted with an unquenchable yearning for love. In both worshipping the Lord who thirsts and tending to those she came to see as Christs in distressing disguise, Teresa took the first steps of a journey that eventually led her a long way from the Loreto compound to the Calcutta slums.

Not long after Teresa took her final vows, life behind the walls of the Loreto compound—and, indeed, throughout all of

India—was disrupted by World War II. For the second time in her young life (she was only twenty-nine when the war began), the normal course of everyday life was shattered by violence. As always happens in war, the poor who live from meal to meal were the most vulnerable.

The city of Calcutta was spared combat, although there were occasional air raids that sent residents scurrying for shelter. But as a British colony, India was expected to contribute to the Allied cause, and many buildings throughout the city, including the entire Loreto compound, were requisitioned by the army. Loreto students and teachers were evacuated in 1942 so that the compound could serve as a military hospital. Most of them were sent to safety in the country, but around three hundred young students were moved to accommodations not far from the compound. Mother Teresa was named principal of this temporary school.

As principal, Teresa was responsible for the welfare of her students as well as the three or four teachers she supervised. But supplies of food, medicine, and basic staples of life were in short supply during the war years, in large part because the Japanese occupation of Burma had cut off essential rice imports. So as food became increasingly scarce, Teresa found herself frequently going to merchants or army quartermasters to beg on behalf of her students. The low point came in 1943, when a colossal nationwide famine, brought about by several years of crop-ruining storms and exacerbated by the task of feeding tens of thousands of soldiers, brought a flood of starving people to Calcutta's slums. To make matters worse, Gandhi, whose moral influence and physical presence might have mobilized much-needed relief, was imprisoned by the nation's colonial authority under the pretense that his years of agitation for Indian sovereignty made him a war risk. With few resources left after the army and government were provisioned, two million newcomers to Calcutta perished.

It was during this time of hardship and famine in a city already swarming with poor refugees that Mother Teresa made a private vow that captured the depth of her dedication to Christ. In April 1942, "I made a vow to God, binding under [pain of] mortal sin, to give to God anything that He may ask [and] not to refuse Him anything."[8] Teresa would never regret this vow, much less shirk or break it. But remaining loyal to it would prove to be more difficult than she could have possibly imagined when she made it.

At the end of the war, when Mother Teresa and her wards were permitted to return to the Loreto compound, she resumed the duties of a simple teacher. But because the principal of the compound school was old and unwell, Teresa continued to do a good deal of the supervisory work she'd undertaken in the temporary school throughout the war years. By all accounts, she was a skilled and tireless administrator.

Social unrest in Calcutta caused by wartime poverty soon began to fuel old hostilities between the city's Hindu and Muslim residents. Throughout the entire nation, relations between adherents of the two religions had been uneasy for some time. But when the British government announced that India would become an independent nation in 1947, the news immediately precipitated a national power struggle between Muslims and Hindus. By early 1946, relations between them had grown so tense that Muslim leader Muhammad Ali Jinnah declared that the only solution was a separate Muslim state. The Muslim League, which he headed, announced a "Direct Action Day," scheduled for August 16, 1946, to demand the partitioning of India into two independent nations, one Muslim and the other Hindu. Gandhi and Jinnah united in urging that the demonstrations remain peaceful, and their calls for the most part were honored throughout India. But in Calcutta, Direct Action Day marches and rallies quickly exploded in riotous mayhem with Muslims and Hindus grimly butchering one another. By the time the violence was finally under control, somewhere between 4,000 and 8,000 Calcuttans had perished, another 15,000 were injured, and some 100,000 were left homeless.

The three days of rioting halted food delivery to Mother Teresa's school, forcing her to brave the chaos outside the compound in search of food for her students. What she saw shocked and horrified her: broken, bloody corpses in the streets, entire blocks of homes and businesses on fire, and frenzied looting. She managed to convince a unit of Indian troops to give her some bags of rice and to escort her safely back to the compound. But the sight of what humans are capable of doing to one another when enraged shook her to her core. It was difficult, if not impossible, to see the rioters as Christs in distressing disguise. Yet Teresa knew she had to try.

The war years, crammed as they were with hard work and scanty food, had been hard on Mother Teresa, and the Direct Action Day butchery was an emotional blow that swept away her last resources of physical strength. Her health began to falter, leading her superiors to worry that she had contracted tuberculosis, one of the many diseases that thrived in Entally. Seeing that she wouldn't voluntarily slow down to recover her strength, the Loreto provincial ordered her to remain in bed for three hours every day. Bound as she was by her vow of obedience, Mother Teresa complied, but she considered the bed rest a harsh penance. A Belgian priest, Fr. Van Exem, who would play a significant role in Teresa's life in the years to come, noted that it was the only time he'd ever seen her cry. "It was very hard for her to be in bed and not to do the work," he recalled.[9]

Eventually, the decision was made to get Mother Teresa out of the unhealthily hot climate of Calcutta by sending her to the Loreto house in Darjeeling, the place where she'd lived as a novice. The ostensible purpose of the journey was the annual spiritual retreat Loreto sisters were required to make. But an additional hope was that Teresa's stay there would renew her health.

She set out for the north, weary but relatively content with her vocation as a Sister of Loreto. But the burden of witnessing the violence, squalor, and misery of poverty for two decades without being able to do much about it caught up with her as she made the train ride to Darjeeling. On September 10, 1946, less than a month after the Direct Action Day massacre, Mother Teresa experienced what she later often referred to as her "call within a call" and her "day of inspiration." It was without doubt the most significant moment in her life, setting her course for an entire half-century.

chapter three

THE CALL WITHIN A CALL

"God was calling me to give up all and to surrender myself to him in the service of the poorest of the poor in the slums."[1]

The journey from Calcutta to Darjeeling was arduous, and began with slogging through jammed streets to get to Calcutta's Howrah Railway Station, itself a beehive of activity. The train's first stop was Siliguri, over five hundred kilometers away. Darjeeling-bound passengers disembarked there and transferred to the "Toy Train," so called because it made the steep sixty-four kilometer climb to Darjeeling on a two-foot-gauge track. Along the entire route, from Calcutta to Darjeeling, there was always the chance that a mechanical breakdown or a heat-buckled rail would cause delays.

There's no record of how long the journey to Darjeeling took, or of how physically taxing it must have been for an already exhausted and ailing Teresa. But what we do know is that at some point in it, on September 10 to be exact, a day annually celebrated by the Missionaries of Charity as "Inspiration Day," Teresa experienced her second calling: to leave the Loreto Sisters and devote the rest of her life to serving the poorest of the poor.

For years, Mother Teresa refused to talk about the experience except to say that it wasn't a vision or rapture, but instead the absolute conviction that Christ—or "the Voice," as she usually called it—wanted her to embark on a brand new ministry. As she once said, "In quiet, intimate prayer with our Lord, I heard distinctly, a call within a call."[2] But, revealingly, Teresa led a retreat for her Loreto sisters immediately after she returned from Darjeeling, and she took as her theme Christ's words "I thirst," spoken to the Samaritan woman at Jacob's well (John 4:7) and as he was dying on the cross (John 19:28). So whatever else the Voice said to her, chances are good that the message had something to do with assuaging Christ's thirst for love and ministering to marginalized people famished for both love and food.

"I thirst" was already an important point of spiritual reference for Teresa before her life-changing experience on the way to Darjeeling, and it would remain even more so for the remainder of her days. After she founded the Missionaries of Charity in response to her call within a call, the words were inscribed in a prominent place, generally by the altar, in every one of the order's chapels. Moreover, on numerous occasions, both spoken and written, Mother Teresa referred to them.

It was only toward the end of her life, nearly sixty years after the Voice, that Mother Teresa finally opened up a bit more about her experience on the train to Darjeeling. In a March 1993 document often referred to as the "Varansi Letter," named after the place in which it was composed, she wrote, "For me, Jesus' thirst is something so intimate—so I have felt shy until now to speak to you of Sept. 10th—I wanted to do as Our Lady who 'kept all these things in her heart.' Jesus' words on the wall of every MC chapel, they are not from the past only, but alive here and now, spoken to you."[3] And in a letter written three years later, not long before her death, Teresa referred to "the strong grace of Divine Light and Love" she received on that 1946 train journey, and affirmed that her experience of "God's infinite longing to love and to be loved" was the real beginning of the Missionaries of Charity.[4]

But what remained private, except in letters to her confessors, is that the interior locutions she first heard in the train continued until the middle of the following year. Jesus addressed her lovingly as "My own spouse" and "My own little one," and persistently asked her to take his compassion to the poor. "Come, be My light," Jesus urged her.[5]

What did Mother Teresa mean by regularly invoking Jesus's thirst? What was the grace-given insight about these words from the cross that changed her spiritual journey?

As a Roman Catholic, Teresa was well aware that all humans, regardless of their station in life, are made in the likeness of God. She was also familiar with the claim in Matthew 25 that whenever we help people in need, we serve Christ. For two decades she had lived in one of the poorest areas of Calcutta, encountering starving, ill, and dying Dalits, untouchables, the lowest of the low, whom no one seemed to care about.

But she somehow hadn't been able to weave all these experiences together until her experience on the Darjeeling train. Suddenly, while deep in prayer, she finally understood that the poor were, as she often thereafter said, Christ in "distressing disguise." Jesus gasped from the cross that he longed for something to quench his physical thirst. Just so, Christ in Dalit women, children, and men thirsted for material aid.

Jesus's "I thirst" meant something else for Teresa, too. It was an expression of intense desire for love and companionship. What's often overlooked is that part of the horror of crucifixion is that it enveloped victims in a surreal and unbearable solitude. The crosses on which they were tied or staked were rarely higher than eye level, so the person nailed on one would've been face-to-face with onlookers who were helpless to rescue or even reach out to touch him. To be surrounded by fellow humans without any possibility of aid from them must have made victims feel overwhelmingly alone.

So Teresa recognized that "I thirst" also signified the longing for love Jesus felt in his final moments, and that Christ in the distressing disguise of the world's poor thirsted not only for material necessities, but even more so for kindness, love, and compassion. Years later, when Missionaries of Charity establishments spread all over the world, including countries whose material standard of living was high, Mother Teresa observed that the thirst for love was felt by everyone, even the wealthy. In fact, she concluded, it was especially pandemic among the well-off who possessed all the creature comforts of life but whose interiors were blighted with a sense of loneliness and alienation.

Her experience of Christ on the Darjeeling train convinced her that it was time to leave the Sisters of Loreto, whose primary mission was teaching, to bend her energies toward serving the poor. But the prospect, although joyful because obedient to the Lord she loved, was also unsettling and even frightening. For Teresa, it was a second painful home-leaving. Working with children made her "the happiest nun in the world," and forsaking it was a "great sacrifice."[6]

Additionally, Teresa worried that her fellow Sisters, not to mention her superiors in the order, would think her vain or, even worse, crazy when she told them that Christ had called her to a new ministry. Six months after her call, she wrote, "From my Superiors down, I know they will laugh at me. They will think me a fool, proud, mad, etc." She declared herself willing to give up her good name if that's what Christ asked of her. But it's clear that she was also troubled by the prospect.[7]

Finally, the thought of living not merely with the poor but sharing in their poverty, as she believed Christ had commanded her, meant sacrificing the small comforts she enjoyed as a Sister of Loreto: regular meals, a settled routine, the satisfaction of teaching children. But as a nun, she was accustomed to obedience, no matter how difficult the task her superiors asked of her. Now it was Christ himself requiring her to embrace genuine material poverty as well as the humility that accompanies it. "I felt that God wanted from me something more. He wanted me to be poor with the poor."[8]

What Teresa didn't count on was the incredible bureaucratic difficulty involved in leaving the Loreto Sisters to work among the poor in the slums. The ecclesial red tape was daunting, and a full two years from her experience on the Darjeeling-bound train would pass before she finally got the permission she needed. It would take a third year after that before her new ministry was officially sanctioned. Teresa, impatient as she was to get started, was sometimes dazed and at other times frustrated by the wait. But she trusted that God would clear the roadblocks in his own good time.

Still, God's will or not, Teresa would've been lost without the aid of her confessor, Fr. Celeste Van Exem. A Belgian Jesuit polyglot in Arabic, English, Flemish, French, German, Greek, Hebrew, Latin, and Sanskrit, Van Exem had come to India because he felt a call to foster Christian-Muslim dialogue. But as things turned out, his relationship with Teresa evolved from being her spiritual director to joining her ministry.

Fr. Van Exem's first response when Teresa told him about her call within a call was to counsel her to take a few months to further discern if her desire to minister to the poor really was God's will. When it was clear that she was committed, Van Exem offered her some strategic advice about how to proceed.

He told Teresa that she could go about seeking permission to leave the Loreto Sisters in one of two ways. She could petition the Vatican directly. That would be the quicker route. But if she were denied permission, that would be the end of the matter, with no chance for an appeal. Alternatively, she could go through the archbishop of Calcutta, Ferdinand Périer, also a Belgian Jesuit. An endorsement by him would go a long way with Vatican officials, and if he disapproved of Teresa's plan, she could try to bypass his decision by appealing to Rome. In either case, Van Exem advised, she would need to be released from her Loreto vows by the order's general superior.

Van Exem strongly recommended the second route, and Teresa followed his advice. He helped her write a letter to the archbishop that described what she hoped to do—she later admitted that she'd never have been able to compose the letter on her own—and gave her good counsel on what to say to Périer if he wanted to interview her personally. In the meantime, Van Exem volunteered to hand-carry Teresa's letter to the archbishop and to advocate for her.

The archbishop's first response was discouraging. Périer was by nature a cautious man, and he wanted to make sure that Teresa's calling was genuine before giving her any kind of green light. He'd been in Calcutta for over four decades and knew how difficult it was to launch the kind of ministry proposed by Teresa. In addition to the sheer hardship of working with the poorest of the poor, there was the disdain felt for Dalits by native Indians. Périer was concerned that a special ministry to them would meet with resistance by the higher castes.

On a more personal level, he was annoyed that a priest who'd been in India for only a short time thought it proper to lecture him on ministry to the poor. "You have only just arrived here," Périer said to Van Exem, "and already you are telling the nuns to leave their convents.... You say this is the will of God, just like that. I am a bishop and I don't profess to know what is the will of God."⁹ Périer's irritation was palpable.

The upshot of the meeting between Van Exem and the archbishop was that no action would be taken for at least a year. Périer instructed Van Exem to tell Teresa to keep her desire to leave Loreto secret, and he commissioned a panel of priests, including Van Exem, to advise him on Teresa's petition.

At about this time, Teresa was dispatched by her superiors to a posting at the Loreto convent in Asansol, a town three hours by train from Calcutta. It's not entirely clear if the posting was coincidental or suggested to Teresa's superiors by Archbishop Périer. Years later, Fr. Van Exem speculated that even though Teresa kept quiet about her new calling, her Sisters in Calcutta sensed that something wasn't quite right with her, and sent her away in the hope that a change of scene would set things straight.

But the order to go to Asansol, while perhaps intended as a punitive measure by the archbishop, turned out to be a blessing. During her six months there, Mother Teresa experienced a series of ecstatic experiences in which she felt united to God. As she later wrote, it was "as if Our Lord just gave Himself to me—to the full. The sweetness & consolation & union of those 6 months passed but too soon."[10] Although Teresa considered these experiences divine gifts, Archbishop Périer, when he learned of them, was unimpressed and perhaps even worried that this troublesome nun was fantasizing.

While Teresa was in Asansol, Périer returned to Europe for a visit, and made plans to consult with two fellow Jesuits about the Loreto Sister's petition. When he told Fr. Van Exem about his plans, Périer was startled to discover that the priest knew both of the men he intended to meet. He immediately ordered Van Exem not to write them about Teresa, lest he interfere with their objectivity.

When Teresa returned to Calcutta after her six months away, she began regularly appealing to the archbishop, who had also returned, for a decision. The two priests he had consulted in Europe, one of whom was a canon lawyer, had advised that there was no immediate obstacle to her petition. Finally, in late 1947 or early 1948, Périer gave Teresa permission to write her general superior requesting release from her vows.

But there was a catch. The archbishop insisted that Teresa ask for an indult of secularization, which would strip her of her identity as a vowed nun in the Roman Catholic Church. She found this demand terrifying; as far as she was concerned, her marriage to Christ that she entered into when she took her final vows was unbreakable. But after Van Exem managed to convince her that her general superior would know what to do, Teresa obeyed the archbishop and asked to be secularized in the letter she sent to the Loreto motherhouse in Ireland. The reply she received in only a month was stunning. "Since this is manifestly the will of God," the general superior wrote, "I give you permission to write to the congregation in Rome and to apply for the indult. However, do not ask for the indult of secularization, ask for the indult of exclaustration."[11]

Even the approval of Teresa's general superior for an indult of exclaustration, which would allow her to leave Loreto but remain a nun, failed to change the archbishop's mind. He insisted that when Teresa wrote to Rome, as she now had permission to do, she request secularization. She obeyed, although with a sinking heart, and Périer forwarded her letter with his own evaluation to the Vatican. That was in mid-February. In the incredibly short period of only four months, Teresa had her response, and it seemed directed by divine will. The Vatican granted Teresa's request to leave Loreto, and sent her both an indult of secularization and one of exclaustration, leaving it to her to choose the one she preferred.

When Fr. Van Exem brought word of the Vatican's decision to her, Teresa was so anxious that she asked for some time to compose herself in prayer before hearing the decision. After he told her the good news, she was eager to begin her ministry to the poor immediately.

There was, however, yet another catch. Archbishop Périer, cautious as ever, told Teresa that he was giving her a one-year trial. If she failed during the probation in her efforts to live with and serve the poorest of the poor, he would recall her to Loreto or even secularize her. But Teresa was confident that she would succeed. For a few rupees, she purchased three cheap saris, white ones with blue stripes, which would later become the habit of the new order she hoped to found. The blue border was chosen in honor of the Virgin Mary.

Even though the Loreto Sisters had sensed months earlier that something was up with Teresa, her departure, when announced, clearly shocked them. Her Loreto superior in the Calcutta compound was so dismayed by the news that she took to her bed for a week. Some Loreto Sisters believed Teresa was being led by God to her new ministry. Others felt so angry and betrayed that they had to be cautioned not to criticize or gossip, but to pray for Teresa and her new ministry. Fr. Van Exam tried to console the sad nuns and calm the angry ones by telling them that Teresa would either succeed, thereby confirming that her ministry was God's will, or she would fail, and consequently return to the Loreto compound.

In mid-August 1948, Teresa took off the Loreto habit she'd worn for twenty years, replaced it with one of the blue-edged saris, and slipped away from the Loreto compound with no fanfare. She was thirty-eight years old, and the most formative years of her life had been spent as a Loreto Sister. Although excited that she was now able to follow the call she'd received on that trip to Darjeeling, she couldn't help being nervous as well.

Realizing that the Dalits she would be serving typically died on the streets because they had no access to hospitals or doctors, Teresa decided that she needed some training in first aid and basic medicine. So she interned for half a year at a hospital run by the Medical Mission Sisters in Patna, a city six hundred kilometers northwest of Calcutta.

Years later, long after there were Missionaries of Charity all over the world, the tale surfaced that shortly after she finished her medical studies and returned to Calcutta, Teresa ran across a Dalit with a gangrenous thumb. Seeing immediately that it needed to come off, she whisked a pair of scissors out of her pocket and amputated it. The shocked patient fainted and fell in one direction, and Mother Teresa, equally shocked by her first bit of street surgery, fainted and fell in the other.

Navin Chawla, an Indian government official who met Mother Teresa in 1975 and became close friends with her, once told her the story and asked if it was true. He remembers her bending double with laughter. "A made up story," she said, but one she enjoyed. "It pleased me enormously," recalled Chawla, "that I had been able to make her laugh so much that day."[12]

chapter four

EARLY DAYS

"I was sure that the Lord wanted me to be where I was.
I was sure that he would offer me a solution."[1]

Archbishop Périer's caution when it came to Mother Teresa's call within a call was frustrating for her, but made perfect sense from his perspective. Throughout colonial India's history, the target of most Roman Catholic and Anglican missionary work was the educated middle class. There were exceptions, of course, but for the most part the poorest of the poor, members of the Dalit caste, were neglected. So for a nun not only to express the desire to serve them but actually to live among them and share their poverty was startling. In giving Mother Teresa a probationary period of one year, Périer in all likelihood believed that her efforts would come to naught, or she would burn out—or both.

There's no doubt that the first months of Mother Teresa's venture were difficult and at times disheartening. When she returned to Calcutta in December 1948 after her crash course in first aid, she decided to make her home in Motijhil, the vast slum surrounding the Loreto Sisters' compound where Teresa had lived for two decades. *Motijhil* means "pearl lake," so named for the polluted horseshoe-shaped body of water that surrounded the slum. There was but one potable water source for the entire area, a hand-cranked sump pump, sewage flowed freely in the gutters, disease was rampant, and thousands of homeless people lived and died on the streets. Thousands more lived in cardboard and tin shacks and begged daily for what little food they ate.

In the first months of her new ministry, Mother Teresa lived in the convent of the Little Sisters of the Poor. The convent was some distance from Motijhil, but Teresa walked it every morning to put in such long days in the slum that she frequently didn't get back to her room until after midnight. She quickly learned something new about the poor who have no means of transportation except their legs. "The poverty of the poor must be often so hard for them. When I went round looking for a home—I walked & walked till my legs & arms ached—I thought how they must also ache in body and soul looking for home—food—help."[2] That same day, she recorded in her diary that "tears rolled & rolled" from loneliness as well as a crushing sense of inadequacy for the challenge she'd taken on.[3]

Mother Teresa was discovering that love in action, as the Russian novelist Fyodor Dostoevsky once wrote, can be a harsh and dreadful thing. But there were also moments of grace that kept her going. One of them in particular remained with her for the rest of her life.

> On my first trip along the streets of Calcutta after leaving the Sisters of Loreto, a priest came up to me. He asked me to give a contribution to a collection for the Catholic press. I had left [the Loreto compound] with five rupees, and I had given four of them to the poor. I hesitated, then gave the priest the one that remained. That afternoon,

the same priest came to see me and brought an envelope. He told me that a man had given him the envelope
because he had heard about my projects and wanted
to help me. There were fifty rupees in the envelope.

I had the feeling, at that moment, that God had begun
to bless the work and would never abandon me.[4]

It took a few weeks for Teresa to get her bearings in Motijhil;
there were so many obvious needs that it was difficult to know
where to begin. She eventually started with what she knew
best: educating children, her primary Loreto ministry for two
decades. Announcing that she would hold an open-air school
for the children of the slum, she was delighted when several
youngsters showed up. Crouching with the children in relatively
shaded parts of the crowded streets, she would scratch letters
in the dust with a stick to teach her young wards the alphabet.
But she didn't limit herself to that. She regularly gave the children good scrubbings and treated their scrapes and scratches.

Teresa had been in the slum for about three months when she
was offered the second floor of a private home as a convent.
The home, located on 14 Creek Lane and owned by Alfred
Gomes, a businessman and acquaintance of Fr. Van Exem, was
closer to Motijhil than the compound of the Little Sisters of
the Poor, and Mother Teresa joyfully moved there at the end of
February 1949. The Loreto Sisters generously gave her a bed,
and she jury-rigged a desk, bookshelf, and altar from discarded
wooden crates.

The following month, more good fortune ended the loneliness that occasionally had brought her to tears: On the feast
of St. Joseph the Worker, Teresa's first companion joined her.

Subhasini Das, one of Teresa's students from Loreto, showed up at 14 Creek Lane eager to join her ex-teacher's ministry. (Subhasini became Sister Agnes in the Missionaries of Charity, and she remained with Mother Teresa for the rest of her life. As she lay dying of cancer in April 1997, an ailing Teresa, who herself had only six more months of life, sat at her bedside.) Years later, Teresa's recollection of Subhasini's arrival still throbbed with gratitude.

> There was a knock at my door. I opened it and stood motionless. My heart beat faster as I looked at the frail figure facing me and heard her say, "Mother, I have come to join you."
>
> "It will be a hard life. Are you prepared for it?" I asked the girl.
>
> "I know it will be hard; I am prepared for it," said the girl. And she stepped in.
>
> Then I turned to our Lord, and thanked him: "Dear Jesus, how good you are. So you are sending them!
>
> "You keep the promise you made me. Lord Jesus, thank you for your goodness."[5]

The following month brought yet another aspirant to Mother Teresa's door, and the month after that one more. Before long, ten girls had joined her. "They took off their expensive saris with great satisfaction in order to put on our humble cotton ones," she remembered. "They came fully aware of the difficulties."[6]

Joining Mother Teresa in her work during these earliest months demanded the sacrifice not only of the aspirants' expensive saris, but often the support of their families. Because all of the girls came from the middle class, their relatives were shamed and angry when they discovered that their daughters were in daily contact with members of the untouchable caste. It mortified them to run across their daughters in the streets, and it wasn't unusual for enraged fathers to disown daughters foolish enough to sully themselves in ministering to the poorest of the poor.

A personal milestone in Teresa's life was reached in 1949: She became a citizen of the country in which she'd spent her entire adult life and which she'd come to love as her own. Additionally, at the end of that year, the probationary period Archbishop Périer had insisted on concluded, and Mother Teresa was free to apply to the Vatican for canonical recognition of her work. Fr. Van Exem helped her draft a constitution for the proposed order, to be called Missionaries of Charity, and sent it and other documentation off to Rome. In early October 1950, Pius XII granted the recognition. On October 7, 1953, the Feast of the Most Holy Rosary, Mother Teresa and her companions took vows, she her final and they their first ones of poverty, chastity, obedience, and charity. By pledging the fourth vow, the Sisters promised to dedicate their lives to serving the suffering Christ by ministering to him in the poorest of the poor.

Mother Teresa wasn't speaking metaphorically when she said that the Missionaries of Charity serve the suffering Christ, and neither were her Sisters. In treating ill patients, many of them burdened by open, maggot-infested sores or wounds, the Missionaries were forbidden to wear surgical gloves because the flesh they touched was Christ's. Similarly, lepers were to be treated with the utmost respect for the same reason. Joyful service was always expected, even when performing the ugliest and filthiest of tasks. How could one be otherwise when in the presence of Christ? The spiritual clarity required to see Jesus in his many distressing disguises was renewed each and every day by periods devoted to deep prayer and Eucharist. Without them, the work Teresa demanded of herself and her followers would have been too crushing to sustain.

With energetic young women to help her, Mother Teresa's ministry began to grow. Her open-air school was soon housed in a building, and after that, year by year, more school buildings were acquired to accommodate as many students as possible. Some of the buildings were donated, but many were acquired through a law passed by the Indian parliament that required the government to construct and maintain structures for every one hundred students.

The Indian government was more than happy to give what aid it could to the Missionaries of Charity. The civil conflict that hit the nation after it became an independent state in 1947, caused by the creation of Pakistan, the assassination of Mohandas Gandhi, and the subsequent war between Pakistan and India over the Kashmir region, had left Indian authorities with little money or energy for much-needed social reform. So Mother Teresa's ministries were generally welcomed, and even occasionally enabled, by the government.

One of the first times Mother Teresa was aided by the Indian government was when she decided that she and her Sisters had to do something for the Dalits who died, forgotten and untended, on the streets of Motijhil. Like so many of her ministries, this one was prompted by a personal encounter. As Mother Teresa told it, "I saw a woman dying on the street outside of Campbell

Hospital. I picked her up and took her to a hospital but she was refused admission because she was poor. She died on the street. I knew then that I must make a home for the dying, a resting place for people going to heaven."[7]

Soon after the shock of learning that the poor had no place other than the streets to die, Teresa rented a hut as a shelter for the dying. But given the huge population of the slum, it quickly became too small. So in addition to requesting that the state, under the school law, provide her with a new and larger building for students, Teresa also enlisted the aid of bureaucrats to find a larger venue for the Missionaries' care of the dying.

They soon found exactly what she needed: two huge rooms attached to a temple dedicated to Kali, Hindu goddess of death and fertility. Although the Kalighat was a popular pilgrimage site for Hindus, the Calcutta officials who offered it to Teresa suggested that the two unused rooms would be ideal for a hospice. Mother Teresa gratefully accepted, she and her Sisters set to work cleaning the filthy rooms, and within a day Nirmal Hriday, or Place of the Immaculate Heart, was up and running.

Initially, and predictably, there was local opposition to Nirmal Hriday by those who feared that it was a front for converting sick and dying Hindus and Muslims to Christianity, and doing so, to add insult to injury, in a space sacred to Hindus. One morning soon after opening Nirmal Hriday at the Kalighat, Teresa overheard some Bengalis complaining in their native tongue about the intrusion of this outsider Christian white woman. She replied to them, gently but firmly, in Bengali: "I am an Indian and India is mine."[8] They were startled to discover she spoke their language.

But the angry suspicion that the Missionaries were offering Hindus a place to die in exchange for their conversion persisted. Sometimes, as the sisters carried dying Dalits to the house, furious Hindus threw stones at them. Not for the first time, Teresa explained that the purpose of the Sisters was to love, not convert. She told them that the Missionaries of Charity "avoid evangelizing through means other than our work. Our works are our witness. If someone we help wants to become a Catholic, he has to see a priest. If there is a religious end to our work, it is nothing more than to bring all those we have contact with closer to God."[9]

At one point in the early days of the House of the Dying, as Nirmal Hriday came to be called, a mob of angry Hindus began throwing bricks and stones through the windows, shouting that the nuns inside were forcibly baptizing the occupants. Her nuns were terrified, but Mother Teresa confronted the attackers, her hands outstretched in a gesture of peace. "Kill me if you want to," she said, "but do not disturb those inside. Let them die in peace."[10] Deflated by her courage, the stone-throwing mob dispersed.

Fortunately, trust was eventually established between the Missionaries of Charity and their Hindu neighbors. It wasn't long before Hindu men and women of high caste were volunteering to bathe and comfort the dying at the Kalighat. Once monthly, a local businessman sent a boy to the house with a box of cigarettes for the patients, and each time Mother Teresa blessed the lad. Eventually the businessman came around himself for her blessing.

Years later, after the tense early days of Nirmal Hriday were long gone, Mother Teresa, finally admitted that her goal was conversion, but not the kind her critics opposed. "I do convert," she said. "I convert you to be a better Hindu, a better Catholic, a better Muslim, or Jain or Buddhist. I would like to help you to find God. When you find Him, it is up to you to do what you want with him."[11]

Teresa's primary motive in opening a House of the Dying was simple enough: She wished to let people who had been marginalized their entire lives by an indifferent and occasionally hostile society to die with dignity in the presence of someone who loved them. "We want to make them feel that they are wanted," she once said. "We want them to know that there are people who really love them, who really want them, at least for the few hours that they have to live, to know human and divine love."[12] The worst pain in the world, she believed, is to suffer the incredible loneliness of being invisible to one's fellow humans.

Another milestone of ministry was reached in the autumn of 1955, when Mother Teresa opened Nirmala Shishu Bhavan, an orphanage located not far from the Missionaries of Charity motherhouse. Because of the slum's high mortality rate, children were frequently left without parents. Moreover, many Dalit women sought abortions, realizing that if they gave birth they'd have no resources to ensure that their babies thrived. Sickly infants were often abandoned by desperate parents and left to perish from starvation or exposure. So the Missionaries of Charity began combing the streets looking for parentless children to shelter in the new orphanage. They also urged pregnant women not to abort by promising to take in their newborns.

Sometimes it was too late to do much for the children except to give them love as they lay dying. But the ones who survived grew strong in body and mind, and Teresa made sure that all of them were taught a trade that would enable them to support themselves when the time came for them to leave the orphanage. Teresa also invited her admirers around the world to sponsor an orphan. Surrogate parents would contribute funds for their "children," which would be banked and handed over to the orphans when they went out into the world.

Given the thousands upon thousands of parentless children in the Calcutta slums, Nirmala Shishu Bhavan was soon bursting at the seams. With the help of the Bengali government, dozens of additional buildings were soon turned into orphanages.

The slum dwellers served by Mother Teresa and her Missionaries suffered from a wide range of illnesses that were directly attributable to their unhygienic and semi-starved life-style, and of course the Sisters themselves were always at risk. One of the worst maladies was leprosy, a bacterial infection that, when left untreated, both maims and slays its victims. During the partition troubles, when entire populations were being displaced because of the breakaway of Pakistan from India, thousands of lepers flooded into Calcutta's slums. Once there, their untreated condition was aggravated by the squalor in which they were forced to live.

Mother Teresa felt great compassion for lepers. They not only suffered from a biological disease, but were also spiritu-ally damaged by society's treatment of them as pariahs. Teresa wanted to do something about both their physical and spir-itual poverty, and began soliciting funds for medicines with which to treat them. One of her biographers recounts an incident in which an insensitive potential donor told Teresa that he wouldn't touch a leper for a thousand pounds. "Neither would I," she replied. "But I would willingly tend him for the love of God."[13]

Mother Teresa realized that there weren't enough hospitals—or, for that matter, physicians—to tend to the slum's leper population. So in 1957 she launched a mobile leprosy clinic, with no less a person than Archbishop Périer blessing the enterprise. A new drug, dapsone, was making remarkable inroads in the treatment and cure of leprosy. Patients could easily take it at home without having to go to the hospital. Soon the Missionaries had a small fleet of mobile clinics in which they delivered the drug to patients and offered anyone, leper or not, regular examinations and medicines.

Even so, stationary clinics were needed to cope with the thirty thousand lepers who lived in Calcutta's slums. Slowly but surely, several of these clinics were constructed to treat the worst cases. But a much-needed breakthrough occurred when the Indian government gave the Missionaries three dozen acres of land about three hundred kilometers from Calcutta on which to build a leper colony where especially damaged patients could go to live and die with dignity. People around the world contributed to build the thirty or so dwellings at Shanti Nagar, the "Place of Peace." Mother Teresa even raffled off an automobile used by Pope Paul VI when he visited India and subsequently gave to the Missionaries, and used the proceeds to build a hospital at the leper colony.

By 1960, the Missionaries of Charity had earned a certain degree of recognition from the world outside India. That year, the US Council for Catholic Women invited Mother Teresa to travel to Las Vegas, Nevada, to speak at the council's annual meeting. There was an unintended irony in an invitation to a champion of the poor to come to a city notorious for its bling. But Mother Teresa accepted. This was the first time she had left India since her arrival there in 1929.

After Las Vegas, Teresa visited New York City, only to be shocked by the poverty she encountered in a major metropolitan area of the world's wealthiest nation. She then flew to Europe, eventually landing in Rome, where she was overjoyed to meet her brother, Lazar. She hadn't seen him since she left home in 1928.

Lazar's life had taken a dark turn in the three decades he and Teresa had been separated. He became involved in politics, declared himself a fascist, fought with Mussolini's Italian forces during World War II, and had little use for the Roman Catholicism in which he was raised. (When it fell to Teresa in 1981 to tell him that he was dying and would soon rejoin their mother and father in heaven, Lazar replied, "If you want to join the family, you go—but I have no desire to do so now!"[14]) But the meeting between him and his youngest sister was cordial. Teresa had hoped that Lazar could somehow arrange a reunion with their mother and sister, but the tight grip the Soviet Union had on Albania made an actual visit impossible.

In addition to meeting with her brother while in Rome, Teresa also had an audience with Pope John XXIII. John had been elected to the See of Peter in 1958. It was supposed, given his advanced age, that he would be little more than a stopgap and easily controlled pontiff. But he surprised everyone by calling for a new Vatican council in which Church leaders from around the globe were charged with demonstrating the relevance of Catholicism to a modern world.

Teresa met with the pope to request a *decretum laudis,* or "decree of praise." By canon law, new religious orders were forbidden to launch a second mission until they'd been in existence for a full decade. In securing the *decretum,* the Missionary Sisters were placed under pontifical rather than diocesan supervision, and would be able to expand their ministry outside India to the poor, the sick, and the dying in foreign lands.

It took another five years before the requested decree was finally granted by John's successor, Paul VI. Immediately afterward, Teresa and her Sisters planted a mission in Venezuela. The Missionaries of Charity had gone international.

chapter five

MANIFESTLY THE FINGER OF GOD
"Wherever there are poor, we shall go and serve them."[1]

The mission to Venezuela was just the first of many more. In fact, the swiftness with which additional Missionaries of Charity houses spread was a bit bewildering. In 1967, the Sisters were invited to establish a mission in Sri Lanka. The following year saw missions in Tanzania, Australia, and Rome, and in 1970 in Jordan, London, and Bangladesh. In 1971, missions opened in the South Bronx and in Belfast, in 1973 in Gaza, and in 1975, Lima, Peru. By 1975, twelve years after the Vatican's permission to found international missions, Mother Teresa and her Sisters had opened thirty-two homes for the dying, sixty-seven leper colonies, and twenty orphanages in a dozen countries. It was their tirelessness in service to God that prompted Archbishop Périer, despite his previous reservations, to announce that "manifestly the finger of God"[2] was discernible in the work of the Missionaries of Charity.

The establishment of missions, regardless of which part of the world they were in, followed a uniform pattern. Teresa sent out her Sisters only if the bishop or archbishop of a diocese requested them. Once apprised of the need, two or more Sisters would visit the potential site to determine how best to serve its people. The Sisters would then buy or rent the cheapest building they could find to serve as a dormitory and chapel for them and a house for the ill, homeless, and orphaned. No location, no matter how remote, was ignored if there was genuine need for the ministry of Missionaries of Charity. As Mother Teresa once said, "If there are poor on the moon, we shall go there too."[3]

In the beginning of their international ministry, the Sisters primarily cared for the materially poor. But they expanded their scope when Australian Archbishop James Robert Knox invited them to Melbourne to work with drug addicts, alcoholics, and troubled teenagers.

Mother Teresa was happy for the opportunity to extend the breadth of the order's ministry by serving those who suffered from psychological problems, such as the despair and loneliness that led to addiction. But she always made it clear to anyone asking for help that her Missionaries of Charity weren't case workers or therapists. The labor the sisters undertook was always for the love of Christ, not for the sake of the work. "We are not simply social workers," she insisted, "but missionaries"[4] —not in the sense of seeking converts to Christianity, but rather as caregivers to society's most vulnerable. As Teresa once said, "Nakedness is not only for a piece of cloth but nakedness is also that want of dignity, that beautiful gift of God, the loss of purity of heart, of mind, of body. Homelessness is not only for a house made of bricks, homelessness is also being rejected, being a 'throw away' of society, unwanted, unloved."[5]

Just as she didn't want her order to be thought of as a social service, Mother Teresa was also extremely wary of adopting practices that risked turning the Missionaries into just another altruistic business venture, what today would be called social entrepreneurship. For years, she resisted regular contributions of money from donors, fearing that their souls would be harmed if they gave funds that they could easily afford in place of more costly labor and love. Once she even rejected a donation from Cardinal Terence Cooke of New York when he offered a monthly salary to the sisters who ministered in New York City. Mother Teresa had a horror of her order getting bogged down by bookkeeping and investments. Even when she gratefully accepted monetary gifts, she did so only under the condition that the funds be spent right away where they were most needed rather than banked to earn interest or invested in the market.

Something happened in 1968 that accelerated the request for missions and dramatically increased donations of money and goods: The British journalist Malcolm Muggeridge interviewed Mother Teresa. The television program, film, and book that were the fruits of their meetings made Teresa an instant celebrity.

Muggeridge was a high-profile journalist and author who was razor sharp, urbane, and famous for abrasively skewering people he interviewed. Although in his youth he'd felt some attraction to Christianity, he didn't think he was disciplined enough to give up a lifestyle that he rightly saw was at odds with the faith. As he once wrote, "I felt it was necessary that my personal life should not be a disgrace to the Christian religion."[6] He was, in every sense of the word, a secular man.

But in 1967, hearing reports about the diminutive nun and her order of Sisters who gladly served and shared the life of the world's very poorest, Muggeridge was intrigued enough to request an interview with her. Teresa had never heard of him, but acquaintances of hers who knew his reputation tried to convince her to turn him down. They feared that he was planning a hatchet job on her. Teresa decided to go ahead with the interview, telling her concerned friends that it was the work, not she, who mattered. If Muggeridge chose to rake her over the coals, so be it. But the interview could potentially be of great benefit to the Sisters' ministry.

Teresa was scheduled to travel to England to meet with a woman, Ann Blaikie, who had organized a "Mother Teresa Committee" to collect funds and supplies for the Sisters of Charity work in India and elsewhere. Once there, she traveled to London for her interview with Muggeridge. To everyone's surprise—especially Muggeridge's—the two hit it off immediately. Muggeridge saw in Teresa a person whose identity was inseparably and genuinely bound up with helping the people dismissed as dregs by society. Teresa, for her part, sensed in Muggeridge a longing for faith that, at the time, he himself didn't recognize.

The televised BBC interview was a tremendous hit, despite the fact that Mother Teresa was clearly uncomfortable in front of the camera and somewhat halting in her responses to Muggeridge. (She tried to calm down by praying the rosary before the interview began.) As she remembers things, "Mr. Muggeridge arrived, sat down in front of me, and started asking me questions. He had a paper with a list of questions before him. He read two of them which I answered; then I went on talking about what I wanted to say."[7]

What she had to say rang true for the vast audience watching the interview. Despite her nervousness, Teresa's authenticity as a woman in love with the distressingly disguised Christ in the world's poor came across like thunder. Thousands of people wrote the BBC to thank Muggeridge for introducing them to Mother Teresa and her Missionaries of Charity, and thousands sent checks. As Muggeridge revealed in *Something Beautiful for God*, a book on Mother Teresa he wrote three years later, the response to the program was

> greater than I have known to any comparable programme, both in mail and in contributions of money for Mother Teresa's work. I myself received many letters enclosing cheques and money-orders ranging between a few shillings and hundreds of pounds. They came from young and old, rich and poor, educated and unedu-cated; all sorts and conditions of people. All of them said approximately the same thing—the woman spoke to me as no one ever has, and I feel I must help her.[8]

Muggeridge counted himself among those touched by Mother Teresa, and the following year he and his crew arrived in Calcutta to make a documentary film about her work there. In visiting the Kalighat and the leper hospitals, in speaking to the dying and the diseased, the orphaned and the discarded, Muggeridge was astounded at how sincerely grateful they were to the Missionaries of Charity for the kindness shown them. For a cynic of many years like Muggeridge then was, coming face-to-face with unadulterated goodness that gives with no expectation of return was a spiritual turning point.

What especially impressed him was the sheer joy with which Mother Teresa and her Sisters went about their ministries. Of course there were moments when they experienced sorrow, frustration, and even doubts. But what sustained them through the dark moments was a love that bubbled over into joy. As Teresa explained to Muggeridge, "A joyful heart is the normal result of a heart burning with love. Never let anything so fill you with sorrow as to make you forget the joy of Christ Risen."[9]

While in Calcutta, Muggeridge not only found himself on his knees praying for the first time in years (and admitting that he found it difficult as well as surprising), but was convinced that he actually witnessed a miracle.

Muggeridge and his producer wanted footage of the Kalighat, the Home for the Dying in which the Missionaries of Charity tended to those who had nowhere else to die and no one else to mourn them. Because the building was dimly lit by only a few small windows at the roofline, Muggeridge's cameraman was certain that film shot in it would be dark and grainy. Muggeridge instructed him to give it a go anyway. When the film was processed it showed, to everyone's amazement, the Kalighat bathed in light.

The cameraman admitted that he had no explanation for the clarity of the film, and left it at that. But Muggeridge, as he said, was "absolutely convinced that the technically unaccountable light is, in fact, the Kindly Light [Cardinal John Henry] Newman refers to in his well-known and exquisite hymn."[10] The love with which the dying were treated by Mother Teresa and her Sisters, a love that reflected and passed on the divine light of God, literally suffused the room: such was Muggeridge's conclusion. "I find it not at all surprising that the luminosity should register on a photographic film," he wrote. "The supernatural is only an infinite projection of the natural, as the furthest horizon is an image of eternity."[11]

Three years after his initial meeting with Mother Teresa, Muggeridge stunned his cosmopolitan friends by announcing that he had become a practicing Christian, and he followed up his conversion with three books about Jesus. Naturally, his conversion disappointed those who knew him as a raconteur and witty skeptic. His turn to religion created such a scandal among his secular admirers that he felt obliged to resign his position as honorary rector of the University of Edinburgh. A few years later, when he was eighty, he and his wife became Roman Catholics.

As the Sisters of Charity founded more and more missions in Europe, Asia, Africa, and North America, Mother Teresa became increasingly aware that if the work was to continue, she and her nuns needed help. There was, for example, some work that men were better able to carry out than women, partly because it demanded a certain physical strength and also because it was performed in dangerous areas. So in 1967, an auxiliary order, the Brothers of Charity, was founded for men who wished to serve Christ in the suffering poor. Soon afterward, Brothers planted missions in Saigon and in Los Angeles's Skid Row.

Prayer had always been important to Mother Teresa and her Sisters. No matter how busy they were, there were set times throughout the day to pause for prayer. As Sisters and Brothers aged and were unable to participate fully in tending the dying or nursing the ill, they could still serve through prayer. So in 1976 and 1979, two contemplative orders for Missionaries of

Charity, one for women and one for men, were established. Another order, this one for priests who felt called to the work of the Missionaries, was also inaugurated.

For years, but especially after the Muggeridge interview and documentary, Mother Teresa had been flooded with letters from laypeople all over the world asking how they could help her and her Sisters. In 1969, the International Association of Co-Workers of Mother Teresa was formed. Its members promised to serve God through free service to the poorest of the poor. They collected clothing, money, and medical supplies for the dozens of Charity missions scattered across the globe. They also vowed to live simply, without ostentation or luxury, so that they might be spiritually prepared to participate in the Missionaries' ministry.

Although the Muggeridge publicity brought the Missionaries of Charity additional funds and helpers, both of which Mother Teresa welcomed, it also shone a spotlight on her with which she was entirely uncomfortable. She was always reluctant to talk about herself, preferring instead to speak of the poor served by the Missionaries of Charity. Generally, to the frustration of journalists, she revealed little about her personal life or background.

But after the interview with Muggeridge, it was impossible for her to avoid cameras and reporters completely. She eventually reconciled to the undeniable fact that she was her order's public face, that the distasteful celebrity status she had acquired had to be tolerated for the sake of the ministry, and that the many awards she began to receive were bearable if accepted on behalf of her Sisters.

The first of these recognitions came in 1969, when Teresa was given the Jawaharlal Nehru Award for International Understanding. She was the fifth recipient of the annual award; previous winners included U Thant, UN Secretary General, Martin Luther King, Jr., and violinist Yehudi Menuhin. Two years later, Pope Paul VI bestowed the first Pope John XXIII Peace Prize upon her. Named in honor of the pontiff who had written the encyclical *Pacem in Terris* and had labored for a thawing of Cold War tensions during the Cuban Missile Crisis, the award recognized the efforts of Teresa and her Sisters to bring the peace of compassion to the world's down-and-outs.

In 1980, Teresa won the Bharat Ratna or Jewel of India award, the highest honor that an Indian civilian can receive. In 1985, she was invited to address the UN General Assembly. In introducing her, Secretary General Pérez de Cuéllar told the gathered diplomats that Teresa in fact needed no introduction. "She is," he said, "the United Nations. She is peace in this world."[12] Two years later Teresa, was surprisingly honored by the officially atheist Soviet Union when it bestowed on her the Gold Medal of the Soviet Peace Committee.

The work of Teresa and her Sisters received its most prestigious award in 1979 when she won the Nobel Peace Prize. It was actually the fourth time she'd been nominated for the award. Each time, Robert McNamara, the Secretary of Defense during the Vietnam conflict who later went on to head the World Bank, had backed her candidacy. As the director of an international institution that grants loans to developing countries, McNamara believed that the Missionaries of Charity were touching the lives of the world's poorest people in ways that financial organizations like his simply couldn't. The World Bank transacted the transfer of money to governments. Teresa and her Sisters bestowed love and aid directly to individuals.

In Oslo, where she formally received the medal that accompanies the award, dressed in her hallmark blue-bordered sari and speaking, as Indians do, in upwardly inflected English, Mother Teresa accepted the award on behalf of the world's poor. Given the stature of the prize, she knew that her audience would be global, and she chose her words carefully. Even so, her speech is occasionally rather graceless from a stylistic perspective. It tends to leap from one anecdote to the next, and sometimes the grammar isn't quite right. But these faults only underscored the artlessness of the speaker, making her message all the more captivating and her work in the world all the more compelling.

Teresa began by reminding the assembled dignitaries that the heart of her faith was the belief that God incarnated, suffered, and died in order to bring liberation and peace to the poor. Jesus, she said, "died for you and for me and for that leper and for that man dying of hunger and that naked person lying in the street not only of Calcutta, but of Africa, and New York, and London, and Oslo." His message was that "we [should] love one another as he loves each one of us."[13] Humans are called to be collaborators in divine love.

But the aid that we extend to the poor isn't unilateral. The poor have much to give us as well: Their patience and gratitude teach us to be better persons. To illustrate her point, Teresa told the story of the time she and her Sisters went to the streets searching for Dalits who were dying alone and forgotten. "We picked up four people from the street," she said. "And one of them was in a most terrible condition—and I told the Sisters:

'You take care of the other three, I take [care] of this one that looked worse. So I did for her all that my love can do. I put her in bed, and there was such a beautiful smile on her face. She took hold of my hand, as she said one word only: Thank you— and she died.'"

On another occasion, Mother Teresa told her Nobel audience, there was a terrible sugar shortage in Calcutta, and it hit the Missionaries of Charity orphanages especially hard. Somehow word of the orphans' suffering got round to a four-year-old Hindu boy. He marched straight home "and told his parents: I will not eat sugar for three days, I will give my sugar to Mother Teresa for her children. After three days his father and mother brought him to our home. I had never met them before, and this little one could scarcely pronounce my name, but he knew exactly what he had come to do. He knew that he wanted to share his love."

She also told the story of visiting the home of a starving Hindu family of nine in order to give them some rice. The mother divided most of the rice between her children, then took a portion and left. When she came back, Teresa asked her where she'd gone. The woman told her that she'd delivered her share of the rice to a Muslim family. "They are hungry also," the Hindu mother said.

Then there was the time that a man who had been paralyzed for two decades, able to move only his right hand, sent Mother Teresa fifteen dollars. His only comfort in life was tobacco. But by sending money that otherwise could have been spent on cigarettes, he willingly gave up pleasure for a full week to help others whom he would never meet. "It must have been a terrible sacrifice for him," Teresa told the Nobel audience, "but see how beautiful, how he shared, and with that money I bought bread and I gave to those who are hungry with a joy on both sides, he was giving and the poor were receiving."

In telling these stories, Mother Teresa wasn't romanticizing the poor, as she's occasionally been accused of doing. When it came to poverty, she was neither naïve nor innocent. She knew that there was tremendous suffering in the world, she realized that much of it was caused by human wickedness, and she'd seen with her own eyes how destitution can turn otherwise good people into brutes. But for her, all people were made in the image of a good and loving God, and therefore carried the marks of divine goodness and love. What she tried to do in her ministry, and what she recommended to her listeners in Oslo and around the world, was to nurture the goodness in people by lovingly serving them.

Physical suffering in the form of illness, hunger, or dying, wasn't the only kind of misery that Mother Teresa and her Sisters tried to alleviate. They also sought to alleviate emotional and spiritual suffering. During her travels in North America and Europe to relatively affluent nations, Teresa was struck again and again by the prevalence of loneliness, lovelessness, and alienation. In her Nobel lecture, she told the story, for example, about a visit to a retirement home that offered its elderly residents every conceivable luxury. But she noticed that not a single one of them was smiling or seemed happy or content. Instead, they congregated in the home's large front lobby to stare yearningly and anxiously at the entrance. Mother Teresa asked a nurse why these people who had so many material comforts looked so unhappy. "Every day," the nurse replied, "they are expecting, they are hoping that a son or daughter will come to visit them. They are hurt because they are forgotten."

Nor was it only the elderly who often went forgotten and unloved in affluent societies. Young people, like those who Archbishop Knox had worried about when he asked Teresa to open a mission in Australia, also felt the sting of loneliness, and so turned to drugs or alcohol for false comfort—tragically, but not surprisingly, since their parents were frequently so consumed by their own misery that they had no energy left for their children.

This splintering of families into individual centers of pain and alienation is dysfunctional in the extreme. Love begins at home, Mother Teresa insisted. Home and family are the twin tutors in love, compassion, patience, and service. The poor developing world knew this, she said, but the wealthy developed world was in danger of forgetting it.

At the end of her Nobel speech, audience members, who had been riveted to the softly spoken words of this nearly seventy-year-old nun, burst into enthusiastic applause. Teresa thanked them, left the podium, and returned to her seat. She looked exhausted and uncomfortable, as if the acclaim was draining her, and as if the only place she longed to be was back in Motijhil, tending to its Christs in distressing disguise. When she returned to Calcutta after the ceremony, she secluded herself in a private retreat to recharge her spiritual batteries with prayer and solitude.

chapter six

INTO THE WORLD

"Should I devote myself to the struggle for justice
when the most needy people would die right in front
of me for lack of a glass of milk?"[1]

The Nobel Peace Prize changed Mother Teresa's life in ways neither she nor her Sisters could have anticipated. It guaranteed that she would be surrounded by a gaggle of newspaper and television reporters whenever she traveled. It meant that the world's religious leaders would admire her, cynical political leaders would try to ride on her coattails by publicly praising her, and poor people from virtually every country on earth would feel such a kinship with her that they would write letters of gratitude stuffed in envelopes that were sometimes addressed simply to "Mother Teresa, India."

It meant, in short, that Mother Teresa now belonged to the world. Her parish, which at the beginning of her ministry was confined by the boundaries of the Motijhil slum, was now without borders, and she was increasingly called upon either to put out fires or to start new missions for the physically and spiritually poor in dozens of countries.

The widening of Mother Teresa's responsibilities was facilitated in large part by her relationship with Pope John Paul II. Teresa had met Pope John XXIII, as well as his successor, Pope

65

Paul VI, when she was still so unknown that he'd mistakenly called her "Mother Teresa of Delhi." But Pope John Paul II, who had succeeded to Peter's throne only a year before Teresa was awarded the Nobel Prize, immediately appreciated her promise as an emissary of Christ's love.

He also sensed a connection between them. Both came from relatively poor families, and both had lost a parent when they were still children. Both had been raised in deeply devout households, and both had discovered their vocation at a young age. Both came from homelands gripped in the iron fist of Soviet-style communism. Finally, both had a deep and abiding love of God and their fellow humans and a special reverence for Mary.

Over the years that Pope John Paul II and Mother Teresa knew one another, their relationship, initially based on respect and trust, eventually grew so close that they felt comfortable occasionally joking with one another—something, given the stature of a pontiff, that seems unthinkable to most of us. According to Fr. Van Exem, Teresa's Belgian confessor, she once asked the pope to help her out of a tough spot. "Holy Father," she said, "so many cardinals and bishops ask me to come to meetings and to speak. I cannot, it is too much for me." Lightheartedly but half-seriously, she asked John Paul II for permission to "tell them that the Holy Father has forbidden me to go." The pope, picking up on the light tone of her voice, smilingly said he'd think about it.[2]

John Paul's esteem and affection for Mother Teresa was also displayed when he visited the Kalighat in 1986, a day that Teresa ever after said was the happiest of her life. When the pope arrived at the House for the Dying, he refused to allow her to kneel before him, but immediately greeted her with a kiss and a hug. Teresa hung a garland of flowers around his neck, but the pope took it off and put it around hers. Then he spent about an hour in Nirmal Hriday, visiting and blessing each one of its patients, helping to feed them, and praying over those who had died but whose bodies hadn't yet been removed. As he was leaving, he spoke to the crowd gathered outside. "For the destitute and the dying," he said, "Nirmal Hriday is a place of hope. This place represents a profound dignity of every human person."[3]

Less than a year after his visit to Calcutta, John Paul II asked Teresa and the Missionaries of Charity to found a second mission in Rome, this one with the homeless of the city's many slums in mind. With generous aid from the Vatican, a dormitory and kitchen were built in an empty courtyard near the Vatican's Holy Office that could feed thousands daily and sleep as many as seventy-five sick men and women each night. When the mission opened, the Vatican released a statement that so beautifully captured Mother Teresa's attitude to the poor that it could have easily come straight from her. "All tramps and vagabonds are welcome regardless of their religion. We do not want people sleeping under the arches of Tiber bridges or at railway stations. People of all faiths—and those of none—will be welcomed in."[4]

The same pope who visited the Kalighat and commissioned the shelter in Rome also turned to Teresa in 1982 to serve as his personal emissary in Lebanon. A savage civil war that began in 1975 between Sunni and Shiite Muslims and Christians had destroyed much of Beirut, a city that for decades had been rightly acclaimed as a seat of learning and beauty. Because it was apparent that the Palestinian Liberation Organization (PLO) was injecting men and materiel into the conflict, Lebanon's neighbor, Israel, kept a close watch on the situation.

In midsummer 1982, Israel did more than just observe. The Israeli ambassador to England was gunned down on a London street by a PLO splinter group. In retaliation, Israel began bombing the area in and around Beirut, rumored to be where the PLO was most heavily concentrated. The bombardment continued for almost two months, reducing huge sections of the city to rubble and taking hundreds of lives.

It was at this point that John Paul II asked Mother Teresa to travel to Beirut, knowing that her years of ministry had schooled her in calming fears and allaying anger. The pope hoped she could do something to bring about a halt, even if only a temporary one, to the vicious fighting that had already destroyed much of the city.

One of the first things Teresa decided to do in Beirut was to visit a Muslim hospice she heard had been hit by Israeli bombs. But what she discovered when she crossed battle lines to get there is that the damaged building was actually a refuge for nearly forty developmentally challenged children. In the fog of war, they had gotten separated from their families and caretakers.

To get them to safety, she had to negotiate a brief cease-fire, no small achievement given the ferocity of the conflict. She succeeded, and so for an hour or two, the bombing and sniping ceased as the seventy-two-year-old nun led the frightened and hungry children through rubble and corpses to a Red Cross camp outside the kill zone.

Over the following years, as Teresa became one of the world's most recognizable religious figures, she and her Sisters visited other parts of the globe where humans were in crisis. In 1984, two years after her rescue of the Beirut children, she traveled by train to Bhopal, India, the site of a gas leak in a Union Carbide pesticide factory that killed upward of 16,000 people. Thousands of other victims suffered either temporary or permanent effects from the leak. The land and water for miles around were contaminated. Crops in the fields at the time of the leak were unfit to eat. So, on top of the medical catastrophe, the leak led to hunger and even starvation.

Neither the Indian government nor the West paid much attention to the Bhopal disaster until Mother Teresa arrived there, examined the horrendous damage, began treating victims, and talked to a few reporters. Such was her power of appeal that things changed almost overnight. The Indian government redoubled its efforts to treat the victims of the leak and feed and house people who fled the contamination. Relief funds and supplies poured in from Western nations.

In 1985, Teresa once again traveled to a trouble spot to bring what relief she could but also, equally importantly, to nudge the world out of moral indifference to the suffering of others. This time she went to Ethiopia, where famine was so widespread that the United Nations estimated that one million people had perished. The following year she traveled to the Ukraine when the Chernobyl nuclear power plant meltdown released a huge radioactive plume into the atmosphere. Her presence there not only helped organize relief for the disaster's victims, but also alerted the world to the hazards of nuclear energy. It was because of her efforts in this crisis that the Soviet Union awarded her its Gold Medal of Peace.

During the final decade of her life, years in which her health was declining, Mother Teresa continued an exhausting schedule of travel, visiting Missionaries of Charity houses, accepting invitations to speak, and going to hotspots around the globe to encourage, by her sheer presence and reputation, peace. Experience had taught her that she and her Sisters were in a unique position to preach the Good News to the world. As she once observed, "This is the wonderful part of our vocation, that as Missionaries of Charity we have created an awareness of the poor in the whole world.... Today the whole world knows our poor because of our work. And they want to share."[5]

In the time she had left, Mother Teresa also reserved a great deal of her energy as well as the resources of her order to caring for AIDS patients. AIDS, she often said, was the new leprosy of the West.

She first took real notice of the AIDS epidemic in 1985, when she received a letter from a Washington, DC, resident that described the physical symptoms of the disease as well as the way AIDS patients were often marginalized by medical personnel and family. In 1985, there was still uncertainty in the medical community about the etiology of AIDS, although it was known to have some connection with sexual behavior. Panic was widespread. In that year, for example, Ryan White, an Indiana youngster who contracted AIDS from an infected blood transfusion, was refused entry to a public school on the grounds that he posed a risk to his classmates. The film star Rock Hudson died of AIDS that same year, shortly before

President Reagan finally acknowledged that the virus was a public health concern.

That June, Teresa flew to the United States capital to visit patients suffering from the mysterious disease. Before the year was out, she had opened a hospice in Greenwich Village. Three of its first patients were Sing Sing prison inmates suffering from the illness. Teresa had appealed directly to New York governor Mario Cuomo to have them transferred to the new hospice so that they could die in peace and with dignity.

When it became apparent the following year that the Greenwich hospice was much too small to accommodate the growing number of AIDS sufferers, Mother Teresa looked around for a larger building. District of Columbia Archbishop James Hickey, who fully supported the ministry to AIDS patients, offered her an abandoned convent as a residence for Missionaries of Charity and a hospice for the dying. There was initial and sometimes fierce opposition to the AIDS hospice from citizens who lived nearby. They feared that they and their children might become infected simply because of their proximity to the patients. But plans for the hospice continued on schedule, and it opened as the "Gift of Peace" in early November 1986.

As more AIDS sufferers were diagnosed at an alarming rate, Teresa and her Sisters responded. Soon Missionaries of Charity hospices were opened in Los Angeles, San Francisco, Denver, and then in regions of Africa particularly hard-hit by the epidemic. Some patients, especially in the United States, didn't stay long in the hospices because they couldn't abide the house rules that disallowed television and strictly limited visiting hours. Others found the general atmosphere of Roman

Catholic piety, complete with wall crucifixes, holy water fonts, and regular periods of prayer, oppressive. But more stayed than left, not simply because they had nowhere else to die, but also because they genuinely appreciated the way in which the Missionaries of Charity tried to make their final weeks as peaceful as possible.

In the last decade of her life, Mother Teresa also became one of the world's most vocal opponents of abortion and all birth control except the rhythm method. This wasn't a new concern for her. One of her hopes in planting orphanages, first in India and then around the world, was to discourage abortion by assuring pregnant women that she and her Sisters were always prepared to take in newborn infants. She often compared the number of people who died in miserable conditions of hunger, disease, and squalor with the number of aborted children, insisting that they belonged in the same demographic because they were all victims of a society that devalued human life.

In her 1979 Nobel Lecture, Teresa took the opportunity to express views about abortion that she held her entire life. She told her audience that just as armed conflict threatens peace, so does the "true war, the direct killing of a child by its own mother"—and, she added "if a mother can kill her own child, what will prevent us from killing ourselves, or one another? Nothing." Abortion, she continued, "is the worst evil, and the greatest enemy of peace."[6]

Predictably, Teresa's firm opposition to abortion and, especially, birth control, brought her much criticism. Given the poverty into which most children in developing nations were born, her opponents asked, how could she possibly condemn efforts to lower their number? Feminist Germaine Greer savagely attacked Teresa in a 1990 article that accused the Missionaries of Charity of refusing to allow pregnant women under their care the choice of abortion.

Nine years later, Greer was still in attack mode. "My only regret," she said in an interview to plug her latest book, "is that in 1990 I did not have the information on Mother Teresa's activities, her political allegiances, her financial dealings, the sub-standard care delivered by her nuns, and her obstruction of other charitable initiatives. Mother Teresa is a modern, media-fed icon, in whose image (as distinct from her reality) the gullible and guilty faithful have invested all their own longing for virtue."[7]

Nor was Greer the only person to look with disfavor on Teresa's moral condemnation of abortion. Three years after Greer's attack, President Bill Clinton invited Teresa to a National Prayer Breakfast at the White House. He urged her to say something, and she spoke for a long time about the sin of abortion—almost certainly not what the president expected. When she finished, the audience response ranged from tepidity to cold hostility. Applause was muted and, at President Clinton's table, nonexistent.

The simple fact is that the better known Mother Teresa became, the more criticism she encountered from people, typically but not inevitably atheists, who disliked what she did and what she stood for. Probably the most vituperative of her attackers was Christopher Hitchens, the Oxford-educated cultural critic and sharp-tongued author who later, along with Richard Dawkins, Daniel Dennett, and Sam Harris, became famous as a member of the atheist quartet dubbed the "Four Horsemen."

In both a BBC program and book, Hitchens attacked Mother Teresa and her Missionaries of Charity from several directions. Although she posed as a tireless servant of the poor, she was actually, claimed Hitchens, a "conjuror" and "trickster"[8] whose real aim was to wage a "fundamental religious campaign" of proselytization.[9]

As if that weren't enough, Hitchens accused the Missionaries of Charity of deliberately refusing the people they took in even the most basic medical care. "The neglect of what is commonly understood as proper medicine or care is not a superficial contradiction. It is the essence of [their] endeavor"[10]—meaning that Hitchens believed Mother Teresa and her Sisters were more interested in urging their clients to die than in helping them to heal and live. The reason? Their aim "is not the honest relief of suffering but the promulgation of a cult based on death and suffering and subjection."[11]

But what really infuriated Hitchens was what he saw as Mother Teresa's cozying up to political dictators and unscrupulous businessmen in order to get big checks from them. He cites in particular her public appearances with Jean-Claude "Baby Doc" Duvalier, one-time president-for-life of Haiti and a thorough scoundrel, and Charles Keating, the American financier who served a ten-year prison sentence for conning savings and loan investors out of millions of dollars in the late 1980s.

Hitchens also attacked Mother Teresa for not speaking out against the brutal communist regime in her native Albania, the self-styled "world's only atheist state," headed by Enver Hoxha. Hitchens was especially critical of her participation in a "Mother Albania" ceremony hosted by the regime, all without a single word from her condemning the thousands of government-ordered abortions and executions, not to mention the material poverty endured by most of the nation's population. This failure to condemn the abhorrent Hoxha government bewildered and enraged Hitchens. "Her homage to 'Mother Albania'—as well as its patron, the pitiless thug Enver Hoxha—invites the same question as does [her] infamous embrace [of Jean-Claude Duvalier]: What is a woman of unworldly innocence and charity doing *dans cette galère?*"[12]

Sociologist Gëzim Alpion, while more even-handed in his treatment of Mother Teresa than Hitchens, agrees that Teresa's failure to condemn the Hoxha regime is troubling from a moral perspective. When asked what she thought of the political situation in Albania, Teresa always replied that she didn't follow politics and knew nothing about what was happening in her native land. Alpion doubts this, arguing that like all displaced Albanians she surely was "perfectly aware" of what was going on, if from no other source than the letters from her sister and mother that occasionally got past Albanian censors to make their way to her.[13]

Critics such as Greer, Hitchens, and to a lesser degree Alpion sense a disconnect between Mother Teresa's actual work and her public persona. Greer and Hitchens insist that the difference is accounted for by hucksterism, while Alpion considers it the inevitable consequence of celebrity.

It's apparent that some of the critics of Mother Teresa and her Missionaries of Charity are motivated by a ferocious hatred of all things religious. Greer and Hitchens fall into this category. But more generally, those who condemn Mother Teresa's ministry insist that the Missionaries of Charity order is unable to bring aid to large numbers of people, isn't as efficient with its resources as it might be, and fails to alleviate pain or heal illnesses in the marginalized people it serves.

Mother Teresa's methods are not faultless. Even some of her admirers are disconcerted by what they see as her order's failure to provide appropriate care for the orphans, lepers, and dying persons the Sisters serve. Collette Livermore is one of them. A Sister of Charity for over a decade who entered the order, she writes, to give all she had to the poor, she eventually left "disillusioned" at what she perceived as the gap between the aspirations and the reality of the order's ministry.[14]

Such criticisms deserve to be taken seriously. Even so, it's important to keep in mind that Mother Teresa never thought of her order as a relief agency. More than once, she asked that people not judge her and her Sisters by standards that, while perfectly applicable in other contexts, don't fit the particular charism of the Missionaries of Charity.

There are two basic approaches when it comes to serving marginalized people. The first is to undertake works of justice by endeavoring to reform social and economic systems of domination that privilege some people at the expense of others. Social service institutions, whether NGOs (non-governmental organizations) or state-sponsored, operate on a large, macroscale, and as such need to be scrupulously efficient to reach their goal of helping as many people as possible.

But as Mother Teresa said many times to advocates of the works of justice, "I do not think the way you do."[15] She and her Missionaries of Charity pursued the works of mercy. Instead of trying to change social structures, they sought to feed, clothe, and love individuals, and that entailed living with those whom they served instead of meeting in boardrooms to study statistics and plan strategy. Mother Teresa, in other words, operated on a small, micro-scale. As she said, "I never look at the masses as my responsibility. I look only at the individual. I can love only one person at a time. I can feed only one person at a time. Just one, one, one."[16]

It mustn't be thought that Teresa repudiated the works of justice or saw them as less important than the works of mercy. They just weren't the way God had inspired her to go. "In the world today there are those whose struggle is for justice and human rights," she once noted. "We have no time for this because we are in daily and continuous contact with people who are starving for a piece of bread and for some affection." But, she continued, "I want to state clearly that I do not condemn those who struggle for justice. I believe there are different options for the people of God."[17] And the Missionaries of Charity chose the works of mercy as theirs.

In doing so, they followed in the footsteps of Thérèse of Lisieux, the Carmelite saint whose "little way" so influenced Mother Teresa. The "little way" holds that God is served in the ordinary tasks of life that we perform if we do them for his sake. No chore undertaken with love is too small or insignificant to escape God's attention. Bandaging the open sores of a leper, holding the hands of a dying woman, feeding a starving man, hugging an orphan of the streets: These are what count when serving God through the little things of life. Quantitative goals are inappropriate. "We have not come here to be numbers,"

Teresa once told her Sisters.[18] "Begin in a small way. Every small act of love for the unwanted and the poor is important to Jesus."[19]

One of the risks of working on a large, reformist scale is that statistics can become so important that they eclipse the flesh-and-blood individuals they stand for. Teresa was grateful for the donations of money and supplies that admirers gave not only to the Missionaries of Charity but to religious agencies whose mission was to work for justice. But she also worried that well-off people never get close enough to the poor, to those who are ill, and the unloved in order to see them as persons. Living with them and tending to them day in and day out rescued the Missionaries of Charity from seeing the poor as anything but lovable humans made in the image of an all-loving God.

It was inevitable, surrounded as Teresa and her Sisters were by so much misery and suffering, that they sometimes became dispirited enough to see their efforts as utterly insignificant. "We ourselves feel that what we are doing is just a drop in the ocean," Teresa confessed. Yet underneath the occasional sense of frustration or even failure was a certainty. "If that drop was not in the ocean," she continued, "I think the ocean will be less because of that missing drop."[20]

What about the charge that Teresa accepted money from dubious sources such as dictators and unscrupulous businessmen? Teresa herself said that she was more interested in what ways financial contributions could help the poor than in where they came from. In part, this attitude reflected her reluctance to judge anyone or write them off as unsalvageable. She sometimes said that allowing the rich to give money offered them the gift of peace of mind. If she was obliged to bring peace to the poor, she surely was obliged to offer it to everyone, including the wealthy.

Still, it can't be denied that Teresa's nonchalance when it came to donations reflected a rather remarkable political naiveté on her part. She simply didn't understand or care to learn more about the world's power structures. "I won't mix in politics," she once said. "War is the fruit of politics, and so I don't involve myself, that's all. If I get stuck in politics, I will stop loving."[21]

Yet is should be remembered that it's this naiveté—or, more accurately, innocence—that made Teresa a wise and good soul who was always ready to forgive others. Christopher Hitchens published his seething critique of Mother Teresa in 1995, but one year earlier he had produced a short documentary about her grotesquely entitled *Hell's Angel*. Upon seeing it, friends from around the world wrote to Teresa to express their dismay and anger. She asked all of them not to defend her publicly. Instead, more worried about the damaging effect his film might have on the people she and her Sisters served than her own reputation, she asked for their prayers. "Pray that that man realizes what he has done, because Jesus said whatever you do to the least you do to him."[22]

chapter seven

LOVE IN ACTION

"Put your hand in the hand of Jesus—
walk with Him all the way."[1]

An Indian admirer of Mother Teresa once gifted her with her own personal "calling card." He was a businessman, so perhaps he intended a bit of whimsy in offering such a worldly item to a woman who had renounced wealth to serve the poor. But Teresa liked the card so much that she had copies made and regularly handed them out to people for the rest of her life.

Written on the small yellow cards were spiritual lessons Teresa had learned from the Church, her prayer life, and her ministry to the poor. She summed them up in five steps.

The Simple Path
The fruit of silence is
PRAYER.
The fruit of prayer is
FAITH.
The fruit of faith is
LOVE.
The fruit of love is
SERVICE.

> The fruit of service is
> PEACE.

From first to last, the spirituality that inspired Mother Teresa and her Sisters was centered on Jesus Christ. It was he whom they heard in silent prayer, he who sustained their faith, he whom they lovingly served, and he who gifted them with the peace that passes all understanding. As Teresa once said, speaking on behalf of the entire order, "My vocation is to belong to Jesus, to cleave to Jesus. The work is the fruit of my love and my love is expressed in my work.... Prayer in action is love in action." The Missionaries of Charity, in other words, aspired to be "contemplatives in the heart of the world," disciplined through prayer to recognize Christ in every person they encountered.[2]

Teresa's understanding of herself and her Sisters as contemplatives in the heart of the world wasn't an identity she developed from scratch. She had absorbed it during her first two decades as a nun, because it's the spirituality of the Loreto Sisters.

Although officially titled the Institute of the Blessed Virgin Mary (IBVM), during Mother Teresa's time, the order was widely known as the Loreto Sisters, named after the shrine in Italy where the founder, Venerable Mary Ward, used to pray.

Ward was an extraordinary woman. She was born in Yorkshire, in 1585, into a Roman Catholic family in a time in which it was dangerous to be an openly practicing Catholic. Her family was well off. Despite their wealth, Ward's grandmother was imprisoned for fourteen years for refusing to renounce her faith. Persecution like this drove Catholic families underground or abroad. Mary chose the latter course, leaving England for the Netherlands when she was fifteen to enter a Poor Clare convent.

Ward soon discovered that she wasn't temperamentally suited for a cloistered life. She yearned to serve God in the world while maintaining the interior calm fostered by the contemplative prayer she learned in the convent. In searching for a spirituality that suited her temperament, she was inspired by the Society of Jesus, founded by St. Ignatius of Loyola only a generation earlier.

The Jesuits aren't a cloistered order. Instead, they labor in the world *ad maiorem Dei gloriam,* "for the greater glory of God," and seek to discern God in all things. Ward dreamt of an order for women who, like the Jesuits, would travel the world as missionaries to spread God's word. The members of this new order would be tasked with the specific mission of teaching the poor to help them attain a better station in life. At the same time, Sisters in the order would lead deeply spiritual interior lives, fueling their good works with regular prayer.

In 1609, back in England, Ward gathered together like-minded women into a community, and it flourished almost immediately. She also formed a similar community in France. The English sisters operated secretly, the French ones openly.

Ironically, it was her fellow religionists, not the English Protestant establishment, who eventually persecuted Ward. Church authorities grew deeply suspicious of a non-cloistered religious community of women, especially one that embraced the spirituality of the Society of Jesus, an order that would soon be persecuted by the Church as well. Ward came under additional scrutiny because she was learned, fluent in several languages, including Latin, in an age when educated women were suspect. In the final years of her life, she was interrogated by the Inquisition and, on several occasions, imprisoned, and the houses of Sisters she founded were disbanded. When Ward died during the English Civil War, still remaining loyal to her ideal of contemplation and action in the world, she must have felt as if she'd utterly failed in what she hoped to accomplish. But she hadn't. Loreto houses endured on the Continent, and before long returned to England.

One of the hallmarks of both Loretian and Jesuit spirituality is the regular practice of discernment, a careful scrutiny not only of the world but of one's responses to it. The goal is to learn to see and serve God at work in the world, even when things seem to be messy or even chaotic, and to distinguish God's will from personal desires. The spiritual clarity sought is cultivated by regular self-examination and contemplative prayer in which one cleaves to Jesus in silence and humility. For Mary Ward, Jesus was the foundation upon which the spirituality of her order was built. As she lay dying, she repeated his name again and again.

It's within this rich tradition that Teresa served her spiritual apprenticeship, and it's also the one that she transmitted to her Sisters and Brothers in the Missionaries of Charity. As she was forever reminding them, "Seeking the face of God in everything, everyone, everywhere, all the time, and seeing His hand in every happening—that is contemplation in the heart of the world."[3] It was so central to the aim of the Missionaries that its requirement was explicitly mandated in the order's Constitution.

> Our life of contemplation shall retain the following characteristics:
>
> —missionary: by going out physically or in spirit in search of souls all over the world.

—contemplative: by gathering the whole world at the very center of our hearts where the Lord abides...

—universal: by praying and contemplating with all and for all, especially with and for the spiritually poorest of the poor.[4]

In chapter three we saw how central Jesus's words from the cross "I thirst" were to Teresa's spirituality. For her, they signified first and foremost Christ's thirst for our love, our kindness, our trust, and our hope, and she wanted that longing of Christ to be the centerpiece of her order. As she once wrote, "the heart and soul of MC [Missionaries of Charity] is only this—the thirst of Jesus' Heart, hidden in the poor."[5] Missionaries were called to so love the Lord that they'd be willing to do everything they could to ease his suffering by tending to the physical and emotional thirst of the people in whom he abides.

Teresa and her Sisters were under no illusion that serving Christ in the poor and the marginalized would be easy. But they were also convinced that the more they sacrificed, the more they eased the pain of Christ in all his distressing disguises. The occasional heartache and more or less permanent physical weariness they took on in the service of others, they believed, was well worth it.

Mother Teresa once expressed this point in a parable so simple that it might have served as a Sunday School lesson, but so powerful that it was wise counsel to her Sisters. "There is a story of a little robin," Teresa told them. "He saw Jesus on the cross, saw the crown of thorns. The bird flew around and around until he found a way to remove a thorn, and in removing the thorn stuck himself. Each of us should be that bird."[6]

But sacrifices made with sorrowful sighs and self-pity, Teresa believed, are worse than no sacrifice at all. The people who relied upon the Missionaries of Charity deserved to be treated with dignity and love, and that obliged Sisters and Brothers to feel and display genuine joy in coming to their assistance. "The Missionaries of Charity do firmly believe that they are touching the body of Christ in his distressing disguise whenever they are helping and touching the poor." How, therefore, could one possibly minister to them—to *Him*—with "a long face"?[7] As Teresa told Malcolm Muggeridge,

> We [Missionaries of Charity] must be able to radiate the joy of Christ, express it in our actions. If our actions are just useful actions that give no joy to the people, our poor people would never be able to rise up to the call which we want them to hear, the call to come closer to God. We want to make them feel that they are loved. If we went to them with a sad face, we would only make them much more depressed.[8]

The Jesus-centered contemplation in the heart of the world that is the spirituality of the Missionaries of Charity demands a life-long process of conversion. As we saw in the introduction, most of us live in me-centered universes. We find it difficult to value other people to the degree we value ourselves. Their needs are secondary in importance to ours, and if push comes to shove, we're pros at rationalizing grabbing more than we can use and leaving them with less.

How does one begin to turn away from a lifetime of selfishness to embrace a vocation of contemplative service? What does it take to convert?

The necessary starting point is a recalibration of one's way of looking at the world. We must recognize—re-*cognize*, come to re-*know*—the nature of reality and the humans who inhabit it. The reason silence was so important to Teresa is because it offers us the opportunity to begin shedding false understandings of ourselves and the world. It clears a space, so to speak, for the recognition that converts. Silence and prayer become the wombs in which we're reborn. They "enlarge the heart until it is capable of containing God's gift of himself."[9]

As we progress in our conversions, the rebirth midwifed for us by silence and prayer nurtures an abiding and grateful faith in the essential goodness of creation and the Creator. This in turn makes us long to protect and preserve the creation, not because we consider it a duty but because our recognition of its divine origin instills in us a loving desire to steward it. God loved creation into being, and we should respond lovingly to it.

This recognition of God's imprint upon the created world, and especially upon humans, made in the likeness of God, in turn prompts us to discern the presence of Christ in each and every person we encounter. That's the contemplative insight that undergirds the activity of the Missionaries of Charity. But what's just as important as seeing God in others is discerning God's presence within oneself.

This is an aspect of Mother Teresa's spirituality that often goes unnoticed, focused as we typically are upon the works of mercy performed by Missionaries of Charity. But for Teresa, it was an essential preparation for loving the Christ in those in want of food, medicine, shelter, or love. She urged her Sisters to "promote and maintain" during their times of deep prayer and recollection "the constant awareness of the Divine Presence everywhere and in everyone, especially in our own hearts and in the hearts of our sisters with whom we live."[10]

Teresa's counsel to her Sisters isn't intended as a therapeutic bit of self-help, although becoming aware of God's presence in the heart can certainly be psychologically comforting and a source of deep calmness. Instead, she offers it as an unavoidable fact about the spiritual life: It's unlikely that we can discern and rejoice in Christ in others unless we also discern and rejoice in Christ in us. The more in touch we are with the divine presence in us, the more easily we recognize it in others. The more cognizant we are that God loved us into existence and sustains us with love, the more readily we know that God has done and is doing the same for others.

Over the centuries, saints in many religious traditions, but especially in Christianity, have taught the importance of recognizing God's presence in both oneself and others. Cistercian monk John Eudes Bamberger, a trained psychiatrist who is also a contemplative, nicely describes the dynamic interplay of this recognition.

He observes that God is discernible everywhere for those who know how to see. But "the most fruitful place to search for God is at the center of the soul of the person you love most personally and so most purely; with the greatest respect for the uniqueness and well-being of that person." Moreover, doing so encourages us to discover "reflexively in our own spirit, the same presence, the same uniqueness that strives to honor the goodness that is the other." Everyone, Bamberger thinks, has an "elusive" sense of God's presence in both themselves and others. But a loving relationship calls forth a lived recognition that makes the presence less elusive. Love "casts a brighter light" that enables us to perceive the "radiance that is at the heart of human life."[11]

Mother Teresa would have agreed wholeheartedly with this observation. After all, as her calling card proclaimed, the fruit of faith is love in action and the sense of wholeness or peace that it creates, in both the individual and the world.

When we arrive at the recognition that we and our fellow humans are made in the likeness of a loving God and hence are lovable ourselves, we may be so overwhelmed with gratitude that we long to do huge things for God. But Mother Teresa cautioned her Sisters, and us as well, that it's much better to do something beautiful for God. This was the advice she consistently gave people who wrote or asked her in person what they could do to contribute to the Missionaries' work.

Doing something beautiful for God didn't require massive reform or overnight changes in social and economic structures of oppression. Rather, it means that whatever one does is entirely and perfectly beautiful if done out of love for Jesus. Contemplative love in the heart of the world is judged by its qualitative accomplishments, not by quantity. As Teresa wisely noted, "It may happen that a mere smile, a short visit, the lighting of a lamp, writing a letter for a blind man, carrying a bucket of charcoal, offering a pair of sandals, reading the newspaper—may, in fact, be our love of God in action. Listening, when no one else volunteers to listen, is no doubt a very noble thing."[12]

In saying this, Teresa was perfectly in step with the Loreto spirituality of finding God in all things, no matter how seemingly insignificant they are. Also apparent is the influence of Mother Teresa's namesake, Thérèse of Lisieux, and her "little way" of serving the Lord.

The spirituality of the Missionaries of Charity, contemplatives in the heart of the world, and its emphasis on the presence of Christ's love in each of us, has sustained hundreds of the order's Brothers and Sisters, and thousands of the people they serve. That's why it came as a shock for so many to discover that Mother Teresa lived for nearly a half-century without any sense of that presence. Yet even though she languished in spiritual aridity, she persevered in her service to God and to the world's millions of Christs in distressing disguise.

chapter eight

SAINT OF DARKNESS

"My key to heaven is that I loved Jesus in the night."[1]

O ne of Mother Teresa's deepest fears after she founded the Missionaries of Charity was that she or one of her Sisters and Brothers would do or say something to cause scandal or detract from the order's mission. In all likelihood this explains, at least in part, her reluctance to speak publicly of the interior locutions she had experienced for seven or eight months after the call within a call came on the train to Darjeeling.

Yet Teresa did cause scandal, although only after she'd been dead for a decade, and then only for a short time. In 2007, a book entitled *Come Be My Light,* which collected much of her most personal and private correspondence, was published, and it immediately caused sorrow and confusion in her admirers and a glee that bordered on what the Germans call *schadenfreude,* taking pleasure in another's misfortune, in her detractors. Her letters revealed that, except for one short period, Teresa had been afflicted with a deep sense of God's absence for the last half-century of her life. Such was her unflagging dedication to the work she'd undertaken for God that most of the world was completely unsuspecting of her spiritual darkness.

On hearing the news, many Christians were confused. What did Teresa's long stay in the spiritual wilderness mean? Was she a victim of depression? Had she lost faith in God? What gave her the inner strength to carry on even when she anguished over what she felt to be God's abandonment of her?

Even Teresa's closest companions in the Missionaries of Charity were bewildered. Never had she made any reference to the darkness except for an allusion that would have meant nothing to anyone but her confessors with whom she shared what she was going through. Four years before she died, she warned her Sisters that "the Devil" is continuously on the prowl in order to "make you feel it is impossible that Jesus really loves you, is really cleaving to you. This is a danger for all of us."[2] None of them could have guessed that the remark was autobiographical.

For their part, Teresa's detractors pointed to the revelations in *Come Be My Light* as evidence that Teresa was a faux-saint whose public displays of piety were hypocritical. Longtime critic Christopher Hitchens declared that the letters revealed Teresa to be a "confused old lady" who had "ceased to believe," and whose service to others was nothing more than "part of an effort to still the misery within." He also argued that the Catholic Church's interpretation of Teresa's time in the desert as a dark night of the soul was a perverse piece of marketing that sought to spin despair as faith.[3]

There's no sense in denying that Mother Teresa's fifty-year sojourn in the wilderness is disconcerting. If God can seem absent to a saint like her, what chance do the rest of us have to connect with God? It's also quite probably true, given the nature of her work among the poorest of the poor, that at times Teresa felt psychologically depressed or burnt out. What normal person wouldn't?

But to conclude that the darkness was the result of depression, much less loss of faith, is to overlook its spiritual significance. Psychological depression is me-centered; the depressive's gaze is always directed inward. Teresa's, on the other hand, was directed outward, to the God whose absence she so keenly felt. Depression renders a sufferer listless; Mother Teresa was always on the go, doing the work to which she felt God had called her. Moreover, dark periods don't necessarily suggest a loss of faith. Instead, they are recognized in the Christian tradition as periods of great spiritual insight although often painful periods of fallowness that prepare us for a closer relationship with the Divine.

Many Christian saints have recounted their own experiences of darkness in their relationships with God, but it was the sixteenth-century St. John of the Cross who wrote what's still considered to be the best analysis of them. Not surprisingly, Mother Teresa knew his writings, and once remarked that even though John's words made her "hunger for God," they also expressed what for her was "the terrible feeling of being 'unwanted' by Him."[4]

For John of the Cross, the *noche oscura* or "dark night of the soul" is a forlorn feeling of being abandoned by God. "Both the sense and the spirit," he writes, "as though under an immense and dark load, undergo such agony and pain that the soul would consider death a relief."[5] The soul suffers most from the conviction that "God has rejected it, and with abhorrence cast it into darkness."[6]

But what feels like abandonment is far from it. The painful sense of being rejected by God is actually a purgation of the senses and spirit that prepares the way for an "inflow of God into the soul."[7] There is no set time limit for a dark night of the soul, although most do not last as long as Mother Teresa's did. Nor does the dark night mean that the sufferer has ceased to believe in God, although intense doubts can arise. In one of her letters, Mother Teresa writes, "In my soul I feel just that terrible pain of loss—of God not wanting me—of God not being God—of God not really existing."[8] But the occasional dreadful thought that God may be a fiction wasn't her primary torment. Her feeling that God had turned his face from her was.

Even if Teresa had never read John of the Cross's description of the *noche oscura,* she would've had some idea of it from her namesake, St. Thérèse de Lisieux, the Little Flower, who likewise suffered from a sense of abandonment toward the end of her short life. Thérèse wrote that "God hides, is wrapped in darkness,"[9] and she accounted for this by arguing that the love of Christ is so overwhelming that its fullness has to be withheld from mortals, a withdrawal that naturally causes suffering.

Mother Teresa's suffering when God hid from her was intense. From first to last, her private correspondence to her confessors attests to that. Just a few passages, representative of the whole, convey something of the loneliness into which her sense of God's absence drove her.

> The longing for God is terribly painful and yet the darkness is becoming greater. What contradiction there is in my soul —The pain within is so great.... Please ask Our Lady to be my Mother in this darkness.[10]

The place of God in my soul is blank—There is no God in me.[11]

In the darkness...Lord, my God, who am I that You should forsake me?... The one You have thrown away as unwanted—unloved. I call, I cling, I want—and there is no One to answer—no One on Whom I can cling —no, No One. Alone. The darkness is so dark— and I am alone.[12]

Before I used to get such help & consolation from spiritual direction— from the time the work has started—nothing.[13]

"The work" Teresa mentions in the last quotation refers, of course, to the ministry to which she was called on that providential train trip to Darjeeling. What especially bewildered and saddened her was that the darkness had descended in 1949, right when she believed she was doing precisely the work God had created her to do. Her loss of the presence of God coincided with the granting of the long-sought permission to found the order that became the Missionaries of Charity. Surely the Vatican's approval was a sign from God that he loved her and wanted her to succeed. But it was just at that point that she felt the door slam shut. God disappeared.

There was to be but one time the door opened in her fifty years of darkness. Pius XII was the pontiff who gave Teresa permission to found her order. When he died in October 1958, Archbishop Périer celebrated a requiem Mass in the Calcutta cathedral. Teresa attended, and on that same day received a respite from her forlornness. As she wrote Périer,

I prayed to [Pius] for a proof that God is pleased with the Society. There & then disappeared that long darkness, that pain of loss—of loneliness—of that strange suffering of ten years. Today my soul is filled with love.

But in just a short time, God "thought it better for me to be in the tunnel—so He is gone again."[14] Teresa would endure the tunnel for the next four decades.

As the years of darkness came and went, Mother Teresa slowly began to see them as something different from the dark night of the soul described by John of the Cross and experienced by Thérèse of Lisieux. It was, she concluded, an essential part of her vocation as a Missionary of Charity.

Even as a teenager back in Skopje, Teresa had longed to serve the poor. When she became a missionary nun, she spent her Sundays roaming the slums around the Loreto compound bringing relief to the poor. When she received the call within a call, she dedicated the rest of her life to giving the poor, the sick, the lonely, and the dying the love that the world had denied them. Moreover, she voluntarily took on their poverty as her own.

Teresa dedicated her life to this work because she believed that Christ demanded it of her. As she so often said, when she succored the poor and the sick, she ministered to Christ in his distressing disguise, the Christ who thirsted.

So it was perhaps inevitable, given that she shared in the suffering of the people she served, that Teresa would eventually discern her own inner poverty as a share in the suffering of Christ himself. She remembered the oath she'd made back in 1942 never to deny God anything asked of her, and she realized that loyalty to the oath meant embracing God's withdrawal.

"We must know exactly when we say yes to God what is in that yes. Yes means 'I surrender,' totally, fully, without any counting the cost."[15] It meant accepting whatever God gave, and giving whatever God chose to take away. And for Teresa, it meant accepting the burden of Christ's passion.

When she was allowed that insight into the nature of her darkness, she recognized it as an inevitable aspect of the call within a call, and would go so far as to say that she actually loved the darkness because it was "a part, a very, very small part of Jesus' darkness & pain on earth."[16]

Teresa's final years, like those of her namesake, the Little Flower, were ones in which poor health and physical suffering became her daily burden. Just a few months before her death, suffering from heart failure and pneumonia, she lay in a hospital bed, unable to speak because of the bronchial tube that had been inserted to help her breathe. She tried to communicate with her caretakers by writing on slips of paper, but was too weak to do so. Finally, mustering all her strength, she was able to scrawl, "I want Jesus." Mass was celebrated in her hospital room and she was able to take a small amount of the consecrated wine.

Those who were with her at the time believed that her request for Jesus meant that she desired the Eucharist, and that's surely a part of what she meant to communicate. But given her decades of living without a sense of Christ's presence, it's not too much to conclude that she also meant she wanted the darkness of God's withdrawal to end. She'd spent over fifty years reliving Christ's passion. If it was God's will that she suffer, so be it. But she longed for it to be over.

And yet, in 1962, in the second decade of her sense of abandonment, Teresa wrote something that anticipated her later understanding of her vocation to suffer the passion of Christ, and expressed a willingness to continue, even after death: "If I ever become a saint—I will surely be one of 'darkness.' I will continually be absent from heaven—to light the light of those in darkness on earth."[17]

This is an extraordinary thing to say, because it suggests that Mother Teresa was willing to relinquish the joy of heaven for the sake of those of us who also lie awake in the night wondering where God has gone. No one would deny that the diminutive nun who served Christ in his distressing disguise for over fifty years deserved some rest. But Teresa thought otherwise. Her lifelong dedication to serving God in his people was, so far as she was concerned, only an apprenticeship for her real work after she died.

chapter nine

SAINT TERESA

"We must never think any of us is indispensable."[1]

Once, shortly after she began working in the slums of Calcutta, Mother Teresa dreamt that she had died. But when she arrived at the gates of paradise, St. Peter turned her away, telling her that there were no slums in heaven and therefore no need of her. An angry Teresa shot back that in that case, she would return to her earthly ministry and fill heaven with the homeless and the hopeless.

She told versions of this story many times, always laughing as if she didn't take it seriously. But in fact the dream revealed something essential about her: As a saint of darkness, she was willing to storm the gates of heaven itself to help the millions of people who lacked shelter, food, health, or love. Like the importunate widow, she would keep banging at the gates until all of her children, as she often called those she and her Missionaries helped, were admitted.

One of the mainstays of Mother Teresa's spirituality was a willingness to suffer in the service of others, to share their material poverty and, as she eventually came to believe, Christ's passion. But in the final decade of her life, ill health was added to her burden of suffering. Years of backbreaking work finally caught up with her, and her body began to give way.

She was diagnosed with heart problems as early as 1989, but refused to lighten her schedule of travel and work. Two years later, after an exhausting tour to the United States and Mexico, she collapsed the day after Christmas with a bad case of flu that turned into pneumonia. While in the hospital, cardiologists discovered that she had serious arterial blockage and performed an angioplasty on her. Had she not undergone the procedure, she most likely would have died.

In February 1992, less than two months after her brush with death, she became ill again and was admitted to the hospital, this time in Rome. The following year she slipped on the wet floor of a bathroom and broke or bruised three of her ribs. Just three months later, she was hospitalized again, this time suffering a relapse of malaria which weakened her already damaged heart and lungs. Despite her age and weakness, cardiologists decided it was imperative to unblock yet another clogged artery.

In 1996, a year before her death, she fell on two different occasions, breaking her collarbone and spraining an ankle so badly that she was forced to use a wheelchair. That summer she was rushed back to the hospital with heart failure. Medical personnel were astounded when she rebounded enough to return to the motherhouse in Calcutta, but the last few months of her life were full of physical suffering. Weakness, heart pain, breathlessness, and dizziness filled her days and nights. Toward the end, she also suffered from periods of confusion. She finally died on September 5, 1997, shortly after making her last public statement, a prayer for Princess Diana who had just been killed in an automobile accident in Paris. Teresa and Diana had been friends for years, and had last met one another just two months earlier.

Mother Teresa was a troublesome patient. She always balked at entering the hospital because of the cost of her treatment, insisting that her medical bills robbed the poor of badly needed funds. Once, she even tried to tiptoe out of a hospital to which she'd been admitted, prompting the matron on duty to caution the ward nurses to keep an eye on her lest she try to slip out again. Nor was Teresa punctilious in taking the medications prescribed for her, and she strongly resisted her doctors' advice to curtail her activities and travel. She had always been diligent in the Lord's work, never slacking or cutting corners. In the last few months of her life, when she sensed that time was short, she struggled to redouble her efforts.

But there was one burden she was entirely willing to lay aside: her role as the superior general of the Missionaries of Charity. It wasn't just that she feared her increasing frailty would prevent her from satisfactorily performing her duties. She also believed she needed to step down so that she would have time to mentor whoever took her place. The order, she insisted, didn't belong to her. Besides, according to its constitution, a superior general was eligible for only two consecutive two-year terms. The Vatican had repeatedly exempted Mother Teresa from this rule.

Once asked what job she could perform for the order if she stepped down from leading it, she replied, only half-jokingly, that she was a skilled bathroom cleaner. But her Sisters had no intention of handing her a mop and pail, and Mother Teresa, despite her protests that she was too ill and old, was reelected yet once more in the 1990 General Chapter. Fr. Van Exem, Teresa's confessor, noted that the outcome pleased both the Sisters and Pope John Paul II. Teresa was considerably less pleased, but accepted the election's result in obedience to God's will. She was at last able to lay down the burden of leadership seven years later in January 1997, only seven months before her death. Sister Nirmala Joshi was elected her successor.

Immediately after her death, Teresa's body was lovingly washed and dressed by her grieving Sisters. It was then transferred in an ambulance with the word "Mother" chalked on its windshield to St. Thomas Church. It was a church in which Loreto Sisters worshipped, a gracious homage to the order in which Teresa had served for two decades.

Because the church was located in one of Calcutta's slums, it was also accessible to the very people Teresa had loved and served after she left Loreto. Thousands of admirers filed past her body to bid her farewell. Some were Christians, but most were Hindus, Muslims, and Sikhs. Teresa had ministered to everyone, regardless of their faith tradition.

Because she had been made an Indian citizen years earlier and was easily, along with Mohandas Gandhi, the best-known Indian in the world, Teresa was given a state funeral. On September 13, her body was borne through the streets of Calcutta on the same gun carriage that had been used in the state funerals of Gandhi and Jawaharlal Nehru. (It must have struck some of the tens of thousands of mourners crowding either side of the procession route that it was as strange for a woman who preached and practiced peace to be carried to her grave by an instrument of war as it had been for Gandhi four decades earlier. Equally incongruous was the gun salute that concluded her funeral.)

One observer of the procession was struck by how genuinely grief-stricken mourners lining the streets were, and with what tenderness they offered Teresa their parting gifts. Sobbing lepers from Titagarh offered their tears, and other groups of India's poorest spontaneously burst into songs of joyful gratitude as Mother Teresa's body rolled past them.

Because Teresa died in the rainy season, her funeral Mass was celebrated in Calcutta's largest indoor stadium. Bishops and cardinals from around the world as well as Missionaries of Charity Sisters were seated next to her coffin, and distinguished visitors from several countries attended to show their respect for the tiny woman who had often exerted more moral influence than they did. Mourners included the Indian President and Prime Minister, First Lady Hillary Clinton, the Vatican Secretary of State, who read a message from Pope John Paul II, and royalty from several countries.

Eulogies were given by representatives of India's different faith traditions, attesting to the fact that Teresa was loved by Christians and non-Christians alike, and hymns were sung in English, Hindi, and Bengali. But it was the tributes of the people Teresa had served that made a lasting impression. An orphan laid a small bunch of flowers on her coffin. The wine, bread, and water for the funeral Mass were brought forward by a reformed prisoner, a handicapped person, and a leper. Teresa's successor, Mother Nirmala, laid an empty chalice before Teresa's coffin, a symbol of the hole that her passing left in the world's heart. Another of Teresa's Sisters placed a pencil, a symbol of Mother's insistence that she and her nuns were but instruments with which God wrote. As she said more than once, "I'm just a little pencil in His hand. Tomorrow, if He finds somebody more helpless, more stupid, more hopeless, I think He will do still greater things with her and through her."[2]

After the state funeral, Mother Teresa's body was borne back to the motherhouse chapel and laid to rest in an unadorned tomb whose modesty is a befitting tribute to the saint of the slums. Pilgrims visit the year round to pray and place lit candles and flowers on it.

Immediately after her death, Teresa's admirers around the world began clamoring for her canonization. Normally a minimum of five years must pass from the time of death before a person can be considered for sainthood, and even that is quick for a Church, as so many have said, that thinks in centuries. But John Paul II, long an advocate of Mother Teresa's ministry, waived the requirement, and the process of collecting documents and interviewing people who could attest to Mother Teresa's sanctity officially began in June 1999. A commission was established to scrutinize the record of her life and the granting of any "graces and favors by God"—healing miracles—through Teresa's intercession.

The process of proclaiming a saint is, and should be, arduous. While all Christians are called to holiness, and without denying that there have been millions of people who have led holy lives without being officially recognized as saints, the Church believes that it is both fitting and instructive to hold before the people of God specific examples of holiness. Consequently, every effort is made to guarantee that the persons officially canonized as saints of the Church are indeed worthy.

The first step, which in Teresa's case was achieved in mid-June 1999, is to secure approval to begin the process that might lead to eventual canonization. At this point, the candidate is recognized as a Servant of God. If there is sufficient evidence to establish that the candidate lived a life of heroic virtue, he or she is recognized as Venerable. Beatification, the next step on the path to canonization, requires at least one thoroughly vetted miracle that can be attributed to the intercession of the candidate, who thereafter is called "Blessed." Canonization, the final stage of the process, requires at least one more miracle. Martyrs, people who suffered and died because of their witness to the faith, are exempt from the requirement for miracles. Pontiffs sometimes waive the requirement because of the extraordinary holiness and achievements of candidates. Pope Francis did this when he declared Pope John XXIII a saint of the Church in 2014.

Sometimes, especially if the candidate for official recognition as a saint lived long ago or in a distant part of the globe, there are few available records to scrutinize. But in the case of Mother Teresa, who had been so active in the world and was so internationally known, the number of testimonial documents that had to be examined was truly daunting. People who knew her were interviewed in Calcutta, Rome, New York, San Diego, and London, and reams of documentation were gathered. By August 15, 2001, two years after the scrutiny began, Teresa's advocates delivered an incredible eighty volumes of material to the Vatican Congregation for the Causes of Saints to study. Each of the volumes was nearly five hundred pages long.

Although no corners were cut, there was never any doubt that Mother Teresa's life, despite the fact that she was not without critics, was heroically virtuous. The more demanding part of the investigation was establishing the authenticity of miracles attributable to her intercession.

Standards for accepting a healing as miraculous are stringent. All reports are thoroughly investigated by a team of medical experts, the Consulta Medica, to determine if something inexplicable by the laws of nature actually occurred. The team members, usually five physicians, will examine patient histories, CT scans, X-rays, and lab reports to determine if an illness was actually present and whether it was cured miraculously. Three of the five must concur before a miracle is announced.

Two of the criteria demanded by the Consulta Medica give a good idea of how meticulously alleged miracles are judged. Healings must occur soon after intercession; too long afterward, and the connection between intercession and healing becomes dubitable. Moreover, in the case of cancer healings, the passage of a full decade is required to make sure that the cancer doesn't return. In general, for a cure to become a candidate for a miracle, it must be physical (that is, not spiritual), follow the intercession as quickly as possible, and be permanent. It's not surprising that over half of the reports of miracles submitted for consideration by the Church are immediately rejected.

In Mother Teresa's case, no less than with other candidates for canonization, many attestations of miracles were examined and dismissed. But one was eventually accepted by the Congregation for the Causes of Saints after being thoroughly vetted.

Monica Besra, a West Bengalian, suffered from an abdominal swelling that first appeared in March 1998. Diagnosed with tuberculosis, she was treated with appropriate drugs that apparently had little or no effect. By August, her belly was so swollen that she looked pregnant and was unable to walk or lie down without considerable discomfort.

On September 5, one year to the day that Mother Teresa died, a Sister of Charity placed a medal of Mary that had been touched to Teresa's body on Besra's stomach. Then she prayed the *Memorare*, Mother Teresa's favorite prayer, several times:

> Remember, O most gracious Virgin Mary, that never was it known that anyone who fled to thy protection, implored thy help, or sought thine intercession was left unaided.
>
> Inspired by this confidence, I fly unto thee, O Virgin of virgins, my mother; to thee do I come, before thee I stand, sinful and sorrowful. O Mother of the Word Incarnate, despise not my petitions, but in thy mercy hear and answer me.

Afterward, gazing at a photograph of Mother Teresa, Besra had the impression that a ray of light emanated from it to her stomach. Later, at about 1:00 AM the following day, Besra awoke in her hospital bed to discover that the large cyst which had steadily grown for the past six months had disappeared. Although there were, predictably, protests from nonreligious people that Besra had been cured by medicine rather than miracle, the Congregation for the Causes of Saints accepted the Consulta Medica's judgment that Besra's healing was miraculous.

On October 19, 2003, six years after her death, Mother Teresa was beatified. The announcement was made by an ailing John Paul II, who himself would be declared a saint a mere decade after his death.

Five years later, a report came from Brazil that a man suffering from cancerous tumors in his brain was healed when his family and priest prayed for Blessed Mother Teresa's intercession. Shortly before Christmas 2015, the announcement for which Missionaries of Charity around the world had been eagerly awaiting was made: The Congregation for the Causes of Saints and Pope Francis accepted the 2008 healing of the Brazilian patient as a genuine miracle.

Less than a year later, on September 4, 2016, Blessed Teresa of Calcutta became Saint Teresa.

Long before she was officially canonized by Pope Francis, Teresa was applauded by millions as the "saint of the gutters" who had dedicated her life to alleviating the thirst of the Christs in distressing disguise throughout the world's slums, ghettoes, hospitals, hospices, and orphanages. She had been a living saint who brought the light of Christ's love to people who felt abandoned and unloved. What made her service even more remarkable was that for fifty years she helped untold numbers of people find God, even though she could no longer sense his presence in her own life. She accepted as her own the suffering and desolation of Our Lord's passion in order to bring comfort to those most in need of love.

And as she promised, this self-described "saint of darkness" will continue to do so.

acknowledgments

I'm grateful to Jon Sweeney, Franciscan Media editor, for commissioning this book and skillfully and sensitively guiding it toward completion. All stylistic and factual infelicities, however, are mine.

I'm also grateful to Francis Xavier Wade, SJ, philosophy professor at Marquette University, who introduced me in 1977 to the life and ministry of Mother Teresa. What he told me then about this extraordinary woman bowled me over, and my admiration for her has only increased in the years since.

EPIGRAPH

1. Michael Collopy, *Works of Love are Works of Peace: Mother Teresa of Calcutta and the Missionaries of Charity* (San Francisco: Ignatius, 1996), 98.

INTRODUCTION

1. Mother Teresa, *Where There Is Love, There Is God,* ed. Brian Kolodiejchuk, MC (New York: Doubleday, 2010), 343.

2. Thomas Merton, *The Seven Story Mountain* (New York: Harcourt Brace Jovanovich, 1976), 237, 238. Italics are mine.

3. Pope John Paul II, "Beatification of Mother Teresa of Calcutta," October 19, 2003. http://w2.vatican.va/content/john-paul-ii/en/homilies/2003/documents/hf_jp-ii_hom_20031019_mother-theresa.html.

4. Kathryn Spink, *Mother Teresa: An Authorized Biography.* Revised and updated (New York: HarperOne, 2011), 181.

5. Mother Teresa, *Total Surrender,* ed. Brother Angelo Devananda Scolozzi (Ann Arbor, MI: Servant, 1985), 15.

6. *Total Surrender,* 120.

7. *Where There Is Love,* 138.

8. Mother Teresa, *No Greater Love,* ed. Becky Benenate and Joseph Durepos (New York: MJF, 1997), 54.

9. Henry Nouwen, *Spiritual Direction: Wisdom for the Long Walk of Faith* (New York: HarperCollins, 2006), 5.

10. *Where There Is Love*, 344.

11. Thomas Merton, *Conjectures of a Guilty Bystander* (New York: Image, 2009), 153–154.

12. *No Greater Love*, 55.

CHAPTER ONE

1. *No Greater Love*, 191.

2. *No Greater Love*, 47–48.

3. Mother Teresa, *My Life for the Poor*, ed. José Luis González-Balado and Janet N. Playfoot (New York: Ballantine, 1984), 4.

4. Spink, 6.

5. Navin Chawla, *Mother Teresa: The Authorized Biography* (Boston: Element, 1998), 2.

6. *No Greater Love*, 192.

7. *My Life for the Poor*, 4.

8. *No Greater Love*, 191–192.

9. *My Life for the Poor*, 2.

10. Malcolm Muggeridge, *Something Beautiful for God* (New York: HarperOne, 1986), 83.

11. Chawla, 4.

12. Muggeridge, 84.

13. Spink, 11.

14. Mother Teresa, *Total Surrender*, ed. Brother Angelo Devananda Scolozzi (Ann Arbor, MI: Servant, 1985), 68.

15. Spink, 11.

16. Mother Teresa, *Come Be My Light: The Private Writings*

of the "Saint of Calcutta," ed. Brian Kolodiejchuk, MC (New York: Doubleday, 2007), 14, 15.

17. *Come Be My Light,* 15–17.

CHAPTER TWO

1. Muggeridge, 84.
2. *No Greater Love,* 194.
3. Chawla, 12.
4. Spink, 17.
5. *Come Be My Light,* 27.
6. Spink, 19.
7. *Come Be My Light,* 25.
8. *Come Be My Light,* 29.
9. Spink, 22.

CHAPTER THREE

1. Muggeridge, 87.
2. *My Life for the Poor,* 8.
3. Joseph Langford, *Mother Teresa's Secret Fire* (Huntington, IN: Our Sunday Visitor, 2008), 56.
4. Langford, 59.
5. *Come Be My Light,* 44.
6. *My Life for the Poor,* 6.
7. *Come Be My Light,* 66.
8. *My Life for the Poor,* 7.
9. Spink, 26.
10. *Come Be My Light,* 83.
11. Chawla, 29.
12. Chawla, 30.

CHAPTER FOUR

1. *My Life for the Poor,* 11.
2. *Come Be My Light,* 133.
3. *Come Be My Light,* 134.
4. *My Life for the Poor,* 9.
5. *My Life for the Poor,* 10.
6. *My Life for the Poor,* 12.
7. Spink, 36.
8. Chawla, 53.
9. *No Greater Love,* 177–178.
10. Chawla, 190.
11. Chawla, 73.
12. Muggeridge, 91–92.
13. Spink, 64.
14. Spink, 185.

CHAPTER FIVE

1. Muggeridge, 104.
2. Spink, 51.
3. Spink, 102.
4. *No Greater Love,* 167.
5. *Where There Is Love,* 41.
6. Dinesh D'Souza, "Conversion of a Cynic," *Crisis,* August 1, 1984. http://www.crisismagazine.com/1984/conversion-of-a-cynic. Accessed January 2016.
7. *My Life for the Poor,* 110.
8. Muggeridge, 31.
9. Muggeridge, 68.
10. Muggeridge, 43–44.

11. Muggeridge, 44.

12. Wyatt North, *Mother Teresa: A Life Inspired* (n.p.: Wyatt North, 2014), 89.

13. All quotations from Mother Teresa's Nobel Peace Prize Lecture come from http://www.nobelprize.org/nobel_prizes/peace/laureates/1979/teresa-lecture.html. Accessed January 2016. The full text of the speech is also in Spink, 323–329.

CHAPTER SIX

1. *No Greater Love*, 152.

2. Chawla, 188.

3. Spink, 178.

4. Spink, 213.

5. Mother Teresa, *In the Heart of the World: Thoughts, Stories, and Prayers,* ed. Becky Benenate (New York: Barnes & Noble, 1997), 41.

6. Nobel Lecture (1979).

7. "You Ask the Questions: So, Germaine, since animals now have rights, how about men?" *Independent*, March 2, 1999. http://www.independent.co.uk/arts-entertainment/you-ask-the-questions-so-germaine-since-animals-now-have-rights-how-about-men-1077925.html. Accessed February 2016.

8. Christopher Hitchens, *The Missionary Position: Mother Teresa in Theory and Practice* (London: Verso, 1997), 15.

9. Hitchens 32.

10. Hitchens 39.

11. Hitchens, 41.

12. Hitchens, 83.
13. Gëzim Alpion, *Mother Teresa: Saint or Celebrity?* (London: Routledge, 2007), 132.
14. Colette Livermore, *Hope Endures: Leaving Mother Teresa, Losing Faith, and Searching for Meaning* (New York: Free Press, 2008), xii.
15. Spink, 87.
16. Collopy, 35.
17. *No Greater Love*, 152.
18. *Total Surrender*, 129.
19. Spink, 88.
20. Muggeridge, 119.
21. Chawla, 210.
22. Spink, 275.

CHAPTER SEVEN
1. *Where There Is Love*, 25.
2. *Where There Is Love*, 156.
3. *In the Heart of the World*, 31.
4. *Total Surrender*, 97.
5. Collopy, 198.
6. *No Greater Love*, 79.
7. *My Life for the Poor*, 15.
8. Muggeridge, 98.
9. *Total Surrender*, 102.
10. *Total Surrender*, 103.
11. James Martin, ed., *How Can I Find God?* (Liguori, MO: Triumph, 1997), 113, 114.
12. *In the Heart of the World*, 39.

CHAPTER EIGHT

1. Paul Murray, *I Loved Jesus in the Night: Teresa of Calcutta, A Secret Revealed* (London: Darton Longman Todd, 2008), 52.
2. Collopy, 197.
3. Christopher Hitchens, "Hitchens Takes on Mother Teresa," *Newsweek*, August 28, 2007. http://www.news-week.com/hitchens-takes-mother-teresa-99721. Accessed February 2016.
4. *Come Be My Light*, 265.
5. John of the Cross, *The Dark Night*. In *Collected Works*, ed. and trans. Kieran Kavanaugh, OCD, and Otilio Rodriguez, OCD (Washington, DC: ICS, 1991), 403.
6. John of the Cross, *Dark Night*, 404.
7. John of the Cross, *Dark Night*, 401.
8. *Come Be My Light*, 192–193.
9. Murray, 83.
10. *Come Be My Light*, 174.
11. *Come Be My Light*, 2.
12. *Come Be My Light*, 186–187.
13. *Come Be My Light*, 161.
14. *Come Be My Light*, 177.
15. *No Greater Love*, 148.
16. *Come Be My Light*, 213.
17. *Come Be My Light*, 337–338.

CHAPTER NINE

1. Spink, 284.
2. *Where There Is Love*, 334.

bibliography

Alpion, Gëzim. *Mother Teresa: Saint or Celebrity?* London: Routledge, 2007.

Chawla, Navin. *Mother Teresa: The Authorised Biography.* Boston: Element, 1998.

Collopy, Michael. *Works of Love are Works of Peace: Mother Teresa of Calcutta and the Missionaries of Charity.* San Francisco: Ignatius, 1996.

D'Souza, Dinesh. "Conversion of a Cynic," *Crisis,* August 1, 1984. http://www.crisismagazine.com/1984/conversion-of-a-cynic.

Hitchens, Christopher. "Hitchens Takes on Mother Teresa," *Newsweek,* August 28, 2007. http://www.newsweek.com/hitchens-takes-mother-teresa-99721.

———. *The Missionary Position: Mother Teresa in Theory and Practice.* London: Verso, 1997.

John of the Cross. *The Dark Night,* in *Collected Works.* Edited and translated by Kieran Kavanaugh, OCD, and Otilio Rodriguez, OCD. Washington, DC: ICS, 1991.

Langford, Joseph. *Mother Teresa's Secret Fire.* Huntington, IN: Our Sunday Visitor, 2008.

Livermore, Colette. *Hope Endures: Leaving Mother Teresa, Losing Faith, and Searching for Meaning.* New York: Free Press, 2008.

Martin, James, ed. *How Can I Find God?* Liguori, MO: Triumph, 1997.

Merton, Thomas. *Conjectures of a Guilty Bystander.* New York: Image, 2009.

———. *The Seven Story Mountain.* New York: Harcourt Brace Jovanovich, 1976.

Mother Teresa, *A Simple Path.* Edited by Lucinda Vardey. New York: Ballantine, 1995.

———. *Come Be My Light: The Private Writings of the Saint of Calcutta.* Edited by Brian Kolodiejchuk, MC. New York: Doubleday, 2007.

———. *In the Heart of the World: Thoughts, Stories, and Prayers.* Edited by Becky Benenate. New York: Barnes & Noble, 1997.

———. *My Life for the Poor.* Edited by José Luis González-Balado and Janet N. Playfoot. New York: Ballantine, 1985.

———. *No Greater Love.* Edited by Becky Benenate and Joseph Durepos. New York: MJF, 1989.

———. "Nobel Prize Lecture," 1979. http://www.nobelprize.org/nobel_prizes/peace/laureates/1979/teresa-lecture.html.

———. *Total Surrender.* Edited by Brother Angelo Devananda Scolozzi. Ann Arbor, MI: Servant, 1985.

———. *Where There Is Love, There Is God.* Edited by Brian Kolodiejchuk, MC. New York: Doubleday, 2010.

Muggeridge, Malcolm. *Something Beautiful for God.* San Francisco: HarperOne, 1971.

Murray, Paul. *I Loved Jesus in the Night: Teresa of Calcutta, A Secret Revealed.* London: Darton Longman Todd, 2008.

North, Wyatt. *Mother Teresa: A Life Inspired.* N.P.: Wyatt North, 2014.

Nouwen, Henri. *Spiritual Direction: Wisdom for the Long Walk of Faith.* New York: HarperCollins, 2006.

Spink, Kathryn. *Mother Teresa: An Authorized Biography.* Revised and updated. New York: HarperOne, 2011.

MORE ABOUT OUR
NEWEST SAINTS
from
KERRY WALTERS

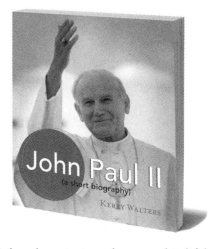

Walters highlights the saint's early years, his lifelong devotion to Mary, his outreach to young people, and his role as a peace-maker with other faiths and denominations.

ISBN 978-1-61636-749-7
$4.99

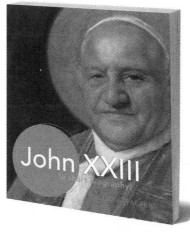

ABOUT THE AUTHOR

Kerry Walters is professor emeritus of philosophy and peace and justice studies at Gettysburg College in Pennsylvania. He is a prolific author whose books include *Atheism: A Guide for the Perplexed, Practicing Presence: The Spirituality of Caring in Everyday Life,* and *The Art of Dying and Living.*